To our friends [illegible]
Always — [illegible]
inspired by
Hope you enjoy reading the book

PERFORM
in times of crisis

CRISTOBAL ALONSO
STOYAN YANKOV

MARBELLA, 13.9.24

PERFORM in Times of Crisis

Written by Cristobal Alonso and Stoyan Yankov
Language editing by Jessica Sandin
Design and Illustrations by Simona Veselinova

No part of this book may be reproduced, stored in a retrieval system, or transmitted in any form or by any means, electronic, mechanical, photocopying, recording, or otherwise, without express written permission of the authors.

Copyright © 2024, Cristobal Alonso and Stoyan Yankov
ISBN: 9798328560498

Contents

Foreword 8

Introduction 11

chapter 1
Building a resilient (startup) culture 17
    Culture matters - especially when times get tough 20
    Building a resilient organizational culture 22
    The resilient culture manifesto: 6 principles for leaders to follow. . . . 26
    Act in line with your values - even more so in a crisis. 57

chapter 2
Planning & effective crisis response 64
    Building strong organizational habits. 67
    Predicting a crisis: noticing risks and preparing to face them 70
    Effective crisis response. 79
    The 4 areas to always keep top of mind 88

chapter 3
Mastering crisis communication 95
    7 essential elements of robust communication in a crisis 98
    PR and external crisis communication 128

chapter 4
Letting people go: the hardest part of the CEO's job . .139
    Accepting that you have to let people go. 141
    The process - who has to go and why. 145
    Communicating layoffs. 148
    Offboarding departing employees 155

chapter 5
Managing your mental state & leading your team......163
Support structures: Equipping yourself to deal with difficulties.......167
Three areas for a leader to keep strong at all times................168
Staying in control in stressful times 174
Leading your team in times of crisis..............................179

Afterword 195
Final Remarks...195
Opportunity-Seizing Canvas: EXERCISE 195
Next steps..197
The authors:..198
Acknowledgments... 200

What readers say

"PERFORM in Times of Crisis is a simple and practical book filled with many examples and relatable stories. It will provide you with guidance and ideas on how to lead in changing times."
- *Howard Behar, Founding President*
of Starbucks International

"PERFORM in Times of Crisis exceeded my expectations. Stoyan and Cristobal's take on preparing for different scenarios with your team is so refreshing. I found it incredibly insightful and a true masterclass in crisis management. Their guidance is both clear and profound, reminding leaders to stay grounded and focused despite insecurities. The practical advice on decision-making and the inspiring anecdotes illustrate these principles effectively. Highly recommended for enhancing crisis management and leadership skills."
- *Kremena Yordanova, Ex. Digital Director at Reebok*

"A great book filled with real-life stories and packed with powerful and useful tools every founder should have access to."
- *Patrick Mork, Former CMO of Google Play*
and bestselling author

"An essential book to delve deeper into our own capabilities as leaders. In particular, I loved the reflections on culture, values, and personal resilience"
- *Carlos Casas, Global Head of Talent*
& Culture (CHRO) at BBVA

"As someone who has led a company through numerous crises, I found the book's practical advice and real-world examples incredibly resonating. The focus on building a resilient culture and putting people first relates deeply to my own experiences, reinforcing the importance of staying true to core values. The actionable frameworks and exercises provided clear steps to not only survive but thrive during challenging periods. This book is a powerful guide for turning adversity into growth, and I highly recommend it to fellow entrepreneurs."
- *Justas Janauskas, Founder & former CEO at Vinted*

"Entrepreneurship is a challenging journey filled with many ups and downs. PERFORM in Times of Crisis is a must-read book for every entrepreneur. It's full of examples and practical ideas that you can apply right away in your day-to-day."
- *Betina Bojniku, Founder & CEO at Visual Narratives*

"A crisis is just another storm that you have to overcome as the ship's captain, and you have to ensure that the entire crew reaches the destination. And that's the hardest part. You'll have to read the book to learn how to perform during that storm."
- *Alexandru Stan, Founder & CEO at Tekpon*

"PERFORM in Times of Crisis is an indispensable guide for navigating the turbulent waters of uncertainty and upheaval. With profound insights and practical strategies, it helps you find the light at the end of the

tunnel to resilience, agility, and success in the face of adversity. I recommend it because every one of us has gone through a major crisis at least once and it's great to have the tools to face it again."
- *Nicoleta Pirvu, Manager at Productivity Mastery*

"5 stars out of 5! I read it with interest and excitement in one single weekend. Cristobal Alonso and Stoyan Yankov put together a remarkable guidebook for everyone going through the upsides and downfalls of building a venture in a high-paced environment. A must-read book not only for every founder but also for C-level individuals as well as venture capitalists to know what entrepreneurs are going through and how to help them in the best possible way."
- *Tomas Cironis, Investment Manager at Ilavska Vuillermoz Capital*

"Stoyan Yankov and Cristobal Alonso knocked it out of the park with PERFORM in Times of Crisis! This book is like having a secret weapon for handling workplace chaos. It's packed with practical tips and real-life stories that make you prepared for handling tough times. Whether you're an executive in a large organization or a startup CEO, you'll find wisdom that'll help you navigate through any crisis. Highly recommend!"
- *Eleonora Petrova, Event Coordinator at Eye Events*

Foreword by Howard Behar
- Founding President of Starbucks International

When Stoyan & Cristobal invited me to contribute with a Foreword for this book I felt it was the right thing to do.

During my time at Starbucks, we grew the company from 30 small shops selling coffee beans to over 15,000 coffee shops all across the globe committed to "inspire the human spirit one cup of coffee at a time". Building a fast-growing organization comes with a lot of challenges.

We encountered many difficulties.

Fortunately, early on, we committed to one principle: to put people first, no matter what. We are committed to people and culture. And we always tried to make decisions driven by that principle. Were we perfect? Far from it. But there's something magical happening when you genuinely care for people in good times. When difficult times come, people will respond with care too.

There are many companies and leaders that say that they "put people first", they talk about it and that never translates into their actions, and their decision-making. Don't be one of them.

The journey of being an entrepreneur is a series of endless challenges. Most of them are small and you go through them like they are nothing. With the challenges come anxiety and stress, but also satisfaction. Our daily challenges excite us and make us feel engaged with our goals and purpose. They test us. They teach us. They make us feel connected to the people around us. Along with the worry these challenges bring passion and excitement.

As human beings, we always like to look for balance. But is there true balance in fact? I always like to think about the image of work as a balancing act on the blade of an ice skate. We're constantly correcting, pushing forward, and righting ourselves. Little and big challenges tilt us a bit or more, and happy endings pull us back. But the point is we are always a little bit out of balance.

We can be tempted to limit our risks by going more slowly or more steadily, and sometimes by hardly going at all. That's when we get stuck in a comfort zone, that may end up being no comfort at all. A retreat to a comfort zone can lead to crisis, just as unplanned risk can.

Sometimes the stakes and challenges are higher. We may feel like our skates are flying out from under us like we're failing with nothing to grab on. Making a decision can be difficult as you keep thinking of the consequences that come with it.

Career planning expert Laurence Boldt talks about this kind of crisis as "a crisis to decide". In fact the Greek word krisis means "decision". A crisis "he explains" often results when we fail to decide on a direction. A crisis compels us to make the decision to commit to a new direction.

A crisis demands the truth to ourselves and to others. It demands that we know and remind ourselves why we're here, what we're trying to accomplish, and where we're headed as an individual and as an organization. When we own the truth, when we're authentic, we have a starting point for facing the choices and decisions we need to make.

PERFORM in Times of Crisis is a simple and practical book filled with many examples and relatable stories. It will provide you with guidance and ideas on how to lead in changing times.

Don't wait for a crisis to happen. Get prepared. Learn what the most effective leaders do. Get inspired by all the examples of successful crisis management as well as from their mistakes. But also remember to listen to yourself. You have everything you need to lead your team in crisis times. Take ownership. Stay true to your values and act from a place of service. Doing the right thing is always the right thing. Enjoy reading this insightful book and as the authors of the book would say "Keep PERFORMing"!

- Howard Behar,
Founding President of Starbucks International
& author of "It's Not About the Coffee"

Introduction

It is mid-2024. The last three years have felt like a constant roller coaster. If you are a CEO or co-founder of a startup, you will have been hit by many different crises: external ones like the different pandemic waves or the war in Ukraine, and perhaps internal ones, like the lack of funding, cash crunches, or your best talent leaving in one go. It seems like an ongoing crisis for which nobody has ever given you a script.

We wrote and published the first PERFORM book during the pandemic. We collected many case studies from startups and put in place a methodology that applies under any circumstances.

P urpose & values
E ffective planning
R oles & responsibilities
F ocus & execution
O ptimal energy
R obust communication
M ental toughness

The PERFORM framework

But as we got more and more feedback from our happy readers, we kept hearing the same chorus: "We've been applying the methodology. It has produced business results for us. But how do we apply it in a crisis?

Introduction

Could you give us some advice on how to lead in uncertain times?" It was constant food for thought.

As our good friend Sergiu Negut, cofounder at FintechOS[1] notes:

"90% of startups fail. It's likely that 90% of the 10% survivors will have near-death experiences. You and I are not the remaining 1%. For you and me, crises are normal. We are not heroes. We don't get any medals. We get to live another day, to face new crises, and to (hopefully) prevail. That's what we need to be good at - much better than anyone else. Again and again."

For Cristobal, 2023 was one of his toughest, if not the toughest of years as a CEO. What he learned over almost thirty years of his career as an executive, serial founder, and investor was meaningful. But he faced new challenges that required extreme mental toughness and a level of energy greater than ever before. New and ongoing prioritization and planning were needed to strengthen the culture and values of his company Startup Wise Guys. Most of it had to be done in real time and had very little margin for error. It required him to become a better, improved CEO.

For Stoyan, 2023 wasn't a walk in the park either. Faced with unexpected challenges personally and professionally, he had to rediscover his own personal leadership. He had to repeatedly take a step back, return to his own values and purpose, and learn to ask for

---

[1] *FintechOS is the global leader in fintech enablement, with a mission to make fintech innovation available to every company. The company was founded in 2017 in London, UK and now has over 300 employees with offices in London, New York and Bucharest.*

help when he was unable to figure things out. He wasn't very good at that previously, as a guy born and raised in post-soviet Bulgaria, where you are supposed to keep strong and resolve things on your own. He learned how to let go, accept, and move on fast when nothing can be done. He had to be positive, and calm and lead his team even on the days when he hadn't slept much, was overwhelmed, and was not feeling very well.

Neither of us was perfect and you won't be either - but we set a clear intention to show up and do our best at every turn.

PERFORM in Times of Crisis

We feel certain that, like any CEO, there were moments in these past months or years when you wondered if you were ready. When we give keynotes and workshops to young and aspiring entrepreneurs, we always finish with a video[2] that rhetorically asks: "Are you ready"?

The answer is that we are never ready for what is coming and what will be required for us to get to the finish line. The real question, though, is: Are you willing? The answer is 100% yes. We are also willing to give you more material, more ideas, and more examples that can be useful during this crisis and crises to come. This advice comes from the heart and our learning from successes and failures. Hopefully, it's advice that is going to allow you to conquer the many challenges ahead.

---

[2] *besomebody. (2016, November 21). You're not ready. But are you WILLING? #besomebody. YouTube. https://www.youtube.com/watch?v=258WM07yssg*

Introduction

This book is the logical sequel to our first book. Just like before, we're sharing our own learnings and advice, as well as our findings from studying successful entrepreneurs and business leaders. Through personal interviews, podcasts, and a lot of research, we've uncovered the very best ideas, examples, and tools to feature in this book. We recommend that you read the whole book to gain a comprehensive, 360-degree view of leadership in a crisis. However, each chapter can also be read individually.

When we started writing, the plan was to structure it into seven parts, corresponding to the 7 PERFORM areas in the first book. Halfway through, however, we realized there are 5 fundamental questions that deserve extra emphasis and attention in a crisis. These questions form the structure of this book, providing you, the reader, with a simple and practical handbook to "leadership in times of crisis".

1. How do you build a resilient culture?
2. How do you plan for and respond effectively when a crisis hits?
3. How do you communicate internally and externally during and after a crisis?
4. How do you manage layoffs and rebuild once things improve?
5. How do you manage your mental state & your team's emotional temperature in the toughest times?

A perspective on "crisis"

The Chinese symbol for "Crisis" is composed of two

parts: Danger and Opportunity.

Danger   Opportunity

In this book, we will provide a perspective on both: how to address the dangers (challenges) and how to keep an eye on the opportunities that may arise. At the end of every chapter, we will share an opportunity story, a practical case from a startup or founder about how to leverage a crisis to create an opportunity.

Paraphrasing our good friend and leadership expert Patrick Flesner[3], "... [these days], leaders find themselves navigating not through the shockwaves of a sudden crisis but rather the enduring tremors of a sustained crisis". To give you a comprehensive overview, we will explore cases and strategies for addressing both sudden and sustained crises.

How do you get the most out of the book?

Read carefully. Take notes. Spot the ideas that resonate. You'll find many cases and examples of strategies that worked for other organizations, but that is not a guarantee it will work in your specific case. Get in-

---

[3] Patrick Flesner is a leadership coach and author of the books: "The Leadership House" and "FastScaling"

spired and find the ones that, with little adaptation, can help you and your team be best prepared to lead in uncertain times. We are cheering for you and we hope this book will arm you with what you need to build a strong and resilient team that cannot only weather any crisis but come out of it in even better shape.

We hope that this book is at least as practical as our previous one and that both, and their tools, enable you to face this crisis and any others that lie ahead of you as a CEO and founder. You are there to lead, to PERFORM at all times, even in a crisis.

CHAPTER 1

Building a resilient (startup) culture

In this chapter:

Culture matters
- Take care of your people and they will take care of the company

Building a resilient culture

The Resilient Culture Manifesto - 6 principles for leaders to follow:
- Inspire Optimism
- Build Trust & Collaborative Spirit
- Invest in Wellbeing & Personal Growth
- Create Clear Structures & Processes
- Embrace Adaptability & Resourcefulness
- Lead with Decisiveness & Courage

Act in line with your values even in a crisis

"True character is revealed in the choices a human being makes under pressure - the greater the pressure, the deeper the revelation, the truer the choice to the character's essential nature."
- Robert Mckee, American author and screenwriter

In our previous book PERFORM: The Unsexy Truth about (Startup) Success[1], we introduced the 3 pillars of a strong (startup) culture: Purpose, Vision, and Values. These 3 pillars are fundamental. Around them, you can intentionally shape your company culture, rather than letting it emerge at random. A powerful, deliberately designed, people-focused culture is key in helping a company through a crisis and should ideally be established before a crisis hits.

- An inspiring *purpose* will encourage action and bring people together when times get tough
- A strong and clear *vision* will help your team stay focused on what matters most
- A team recruited in line with and signed up to your company *values* will operate more smoothly and cohesively

At Startup Wise Guys[2], we always schedule PERFORM workshops with Stoyan during the first week of every acceleration program, immediately after we commit investment. We want to send a clear message that these culture-related conversations are fundamental from day one. Many founders, however, don't take the time to shape their culture or don't do it well enough. Because they didn't shape their culture when times were good, difficult times became far harder to

---

[1] "PERFORM: The Unsexy Truth about (Startup) Success" was published in 2020. It includes practical strategies and examples to help you craft your company culture.

[2] The acceleration program of Startup Wise Guys invests in 8-12 startups from a particular vertical and offers very hands-on support for the first 6 months. Recently, this program started to combine onsite sessions in a designated city with online interactions.

navigate.

In this chapter, we will explore how to build a culture that is resilient enough to take you through the deepest crises and successfully come through to the other side.

Culture matters - especially when times get tough

Difficulties are a guarantee in a startup life. We don't know a single successful startup that has not gone through several tough periods, alongside all the daily challenges. Many startups face near-bankruptcy at some point and have to make difficult decisions. We also know from personal experience that in these situations, it's your culture that will keep you, your team and the company going. Imagine informing employees that you may not be able to pay salaries for the next two months. In a company with a culture they don't connect to, people might immediately start looking for a job elsewhere. However, if you've consistently invested in your people by creating a nurturing and supportive environment, they will help you get through critical periods.

Take care of your people and they will take care of you: BazaIT[3]

BazaIT is one of the top IT recruitment startups in Ukraine. The founders Viktoria Nalyvaiko and Oksana

---

[3] *BazaIT is an IT recruiting platform from Ukraine that creates a network for people who want to get a new job and grow in Tech. BazaIT was founded in 2021 in Kiev, Ukraine.*

Gorbunova believe in the power of a strong culture and treating people well. When they started the company, their first task was to define their values and purpose - even before setting their strategy. Putting people first and creating a nurturing environment was a number one priority for BazaIT.

On Feb 24, 2022, Russia invaded Ukraine. Viktoria and Oksana decided to release the first version of their platform for free, to support Ukrainian startups in these difficult times.

In 2023 the second version of the platform was ready for launch. Unfortunately, the first version hadn't gained traction as fast as they hoped. With funding stalling, managing the cash flow became problematic. Survival was on the line and the two founders had to take drastic measures.

One thing was clear: they didn't want to let anyone go. Instead, they came up with a new plan. Everyone's focus was to help increase sales. In order to make the numbers, salaries had to be decreased significantly.

"We had Zoom calls with each team member, explaining the situation in detail," says Oksana. *"We offered people a basic salary for the following 3 months and shared with them we will understand if they decide to look for a job elsewhere. It was painful."*

Everyone but one employee decided to stay and fight. Thanks to the company's people-first work culture, BazaIt team members were happy to support the company during the crisis. The team was fully aware of the situation and knew that this was a critical point for the company. *"We always believed people are our most important asset"*, says Viktoria. *"We don't do micromanagement in our company. We try to help everyone at all times, providing them with mentoring, support, and opportunities to grow. And I believe this is a big part of the reason everyone showed up in the difficult times we had to go through".*

Fast forward to 2024, and sales have increased. The team is going strong and thanks to the team effort, BazaIt is on track to soon get back to pre-crisis salary levels, with many new opportunities ahead for the team.

Such experiences can either be devastating or the most powerful of your startup CEO career. By emphasizing the importance of the team and shared purpose, startups can help team members focus on the bigger picture and work towards a common goal, even when faced with difficult situations. At the same time, the way you make decisions in a crisis - and the decisions you make - will demonstrate whether your values are real and valid in all situations.

Building a resilient organizational culture

Organizational resilience can be defined as "the business capacity to anticipate, plan, and respond to difficulties when they occur"[4]. A startup that cultivates a resilient organizational culture has an edge in a world filled with changes and uncertainties.

---

[4] *Herman, M. (2022, November 24). 5 Starting points for a resilient organizational culture. LumApps. https://www.lumapps.com/employee-experience/resilient-organizational-culture/*

According to McKinsey & Co.[5]: "Resilient organizations don't just bounce back from misfortune or change; they bounce forward. They absorb the shocks and turn them into opportunities to capture sustainable, inclusive growth. When challenges emerge, leaders and teams in resilient organizations quickly assess the situation, reorient themselves, double down on what's working, and walk away from what's not."

So, how do we build a resilient culture? Where do we begin? According to PhD George Stalk Jr., writing in Harvard Business Review[6]: "A culture of organizational resilience is built largely upon leadership, what we refer to as "resilient leadership." Consistent with the "Law of the Few" described in Malcolm Gladwell's book, The Tipping Point, we believe key leadership personnel, often frontline leadership, appear to have the ability to "tip" the organization in the direction of resilience and to serve as a catalyst to increase group cohesion and dedication to the mission."

Your actions will determine the tone of your culture - in particular the actions you take when things aren't going well because this is when it matters most. Let's reflect:

- How did you act when times were tough?
- Did you make decisions in line with your company values?

---

[5] *Maor, D., Park, M., & Weddle, B. (2022, October 12). Raising the resilience of your organization. McKinsey & Company.* https://www.mckinsey.com/capabilities/people-and-organizational-performance/our-insights/raising-the-resilience-of-your-organization

[6] *Everly, G. S., Jr. (2014, July 23). Building a resilient organizational culture. Harvard Business Review.* https://hbr.org/2011/06/building-a-resilient-organizat

- Did you do your best to prepare for upcoming difficulties?
- Were you quick to address the most pressing challenges?
- Were you supportive and encouraging to your team and your co-founders?
- Would you recommend yourself as an example and role model whose behavior your team should follow?
- Which of your character traits would you like to improve going forward?

Every action and decision you make can leave an impact on your company and team culture. If it gets repeated or encouraged enough, it will be established as the norm.

> "If you only write down your values and principles, you will get almost no value from them. If you print them or post them somewhere in your office, you will still get little value from them. To create real impact you must ritualize how they are created."
> - *Patrick Bet David, Choose your Enemies Wisely* [7]

Rituals, practices, and organizational habits can help you cultivate your culture. As a leader, you are like a gardener. Your (startup) culture is your garden, with your team members as the trees - fundamental to the overall success. Regardless of the garden's potential,

---

[7] *Bet-David, P. (2023). Choose your enemies wisely: Business Planning for the Audacious Few. Penguin.*

planting the right trees is crucial for yielding great harvests. Bringing in the right people is the primary factor in cultivating a fruitful environment, but it's not the sole factor. Trees need sunlight for proper growth and your team members will blossom with appreciation, praise, and encouragement. Occasionally, you might need to trim certain branches, removing undesirable elements to ensure the good parts grow. This means addressing unacceptable behaviors or breaches of values within the team. For your garden to thrive, consistent care is necessary. Regularly water and fertilize the trees, remove weeds and bugs, and reap the benefits of your efforts.

As you can see, it is crucial to be intentional about your organization's culture - and in an environment with difficult challenges, you must have a resilient organizational culture. But what does building a resilient culture mean in practice?

The resilient culture manifesto: 6 principles for leaders to follow

1. **Inspire Optimism**

    A resilient culture embraces positivity and optimism. When a crisis hits, it can be easy for stress and negativity to prevail, but a 'glass-half-empty" mindset can be detrimental when times are hard. It's important to have the mentality of bouncing back to positivity as fast as possible and focus on resolving the current situation. A leader should plant the seeds of optimism at any opportunity: in a team meeting, news update, or casual conversation. If people do not believe that the challenges can be resolved, there's no reason for them to try. Optimism can be fuelled by practices and rituals, and modeled by leaders' behavior.

Showing gratitude: Startup Wise Guys and Cosmic Centaurs

In the early days of the pandemic and during the first days of the war in Ukraine, it wasn't easy to keep the weekly Startup Wise Guys team calls upbeat and positive. Too many people were affected or emotional. The team decided to implement a new element at the end of their weekly team calls: "Thank you time". It's a chance to show gratitude to those who did something special to help others in the team. This simple practice helps the team to focus on the positive, regardless of how difficult the external news and updates are.

Cosmic Centaurs[8] has a similar practice. They call it #GratitudeJar - a dedicated Slack Channel where each team member shares feedback from their clients and community. This special jar holds kind words, feedback, and experiences they all hold very close to their hearts. It is their way of holding on to the special moments in their journey. *"When I feel tired or low on motivation, I look at it and it re-energizes me,"* says founder and CEO Marilyn Zakhour. *"In fact a 2007 study in the Journal of Social and Clinical Psychology shows that grateful people cope with stress in healthy ways and we definitely feel that when we peek into our jar."*

What practices can you include in your own culture?

A culture of optimism of course shouldn't be delusional, where everything is pink and shiny with uni-

---

[8] Cosmic Centaurs is a consultancy, training, technology, and insights company helping executives, leaders, managers, and teams, creating happier and more flexible workplaces. Founded in Dubai, United Arab Emirates in 2020

corns flying in the sky. There is a term that describes this perfectly: Bounded optimism. It is defined as: "The will to move forward with hope to a new reality–all while accepting the current reality"[9].

But optimism vs pessimism is not an even game. Humans have a negativity bias.

Imagine you post a video online. You receive dozens of positive comments and one negative post, criticizing you directly. Which one do you remember? Of course.

"The negativity bias is our tendency not only to register negative stimuli more readily but also to dwell on these events"[10]. In other words, we tend to make problems bigger than they are. In a crisis, there is plenty of negative news and bad things that hijack your focus, so

---

[9] Brassey, J., & Kruyt, M. (2020, April 30). How to demonstrate calm and optimism in a crisis. McKinsey & Company. https://www.mckinsey.com/capabilities/people-and-organizational-performance/our-insights/how-to-demonstrate-calm-and-optimism-in-a-crisis

[10] MSEd, K. C. (2023, November 13). What is the negativity bias? Verywell Mind. https://www.verywellmind.com/negative-bias-4589618

you need to double down on the positive. Build that muscle and inspire your team to do the same.

Celebrate your achievements, small or big. Don't forget to share good news and improvements, especially in bad times. Show up with enthusiasm and positive energy. When you hire a new employee, make sure that on top of their skills and experience, they are a genuinely optimistic person.

Humor is an excellent tool to help you endure difficulties. Cristobal and Stoyan strongly believe in the power of humor, play, and fun. Stress and anxiety decrease after a good joke. Humor can also bring people together. Laughter provides a bonding experience. Laughing at the difficulties and not taking ourselves "too seriously" helps us be more focused on resolving problems.

Here's what Lubomila Jordanova, Founder & CEO at Plan A for the Planet[11] told us:

"I laugh a lot with my team. For me, making jokes is literally part of my job. I feel like it's a necessity if you want to make sure people know that whatever the challenge, we are going to fix it, we are going to figure it out."

---

[11] *Plan A for the Planet is Europe's leading corporate carbon accounting, decarbonisation, and ESG reporting software provider. It was founded in 2017 in Berlin, Germany.*

2. Build Trust & Collaborative Spirit

In his book "The Five Dysfunctions of a Team", author Patrick Lencioni placed "Absence of Trust" as the fundamental issue. All other dysfunctions pile on top of it. Trust is the base for everything in a team. It can be very difficult to build and very easy to lose. A team operating with high levels of trust has a higher chance of performing well in a crisis. In Chapter 3, we discuss the role of trust when communicating in a crisis.

In a professional context, trust is built on four pillars:

1. Honesty
I trust you will tell me the truth. You will be honest and open even if what you are saying isn't pleasant.

2. Competence
I trust you have the capability, experience, and skill set to complete a task or project.

3. Ownership
I trust you will deliver what has been promised within the deadline and to the expected quality.

4. Care
I trust that you genuinely care and you act in accordance with our team values.

Think about it. When you didn't trust someone in the past, what was the reason?

Which of the four pillars was missing? Thinking about your current team: are you ready to go to battle with them? Do you trust them? If there are doubts, where are these coming from?

To cultivate a culture of trust, you have to be a trustworthy leader:

• Show up authentically. Be direct. Share news and updates regularly and bluntly - and that includes your own failures and mistakes. Have regular conversations with your team. Create feedback sessions. Make sure everyone is comfortable with sharing constructive feedback and pointing out what's not working well.

• Demand high standards of competence and skill Don't try to be an expert at everything. You are not. Admit your shortcomings and delegate effectively. Be extremely good in your own roles and responsibilities - keep learning and getting better. If people aren't performing well in their own roles, don't ignore it. Address it immediately. A-players get frustrated when they have to work with people who are poor performers. That's not to say you shouldn't hire less experienced people, with talent and potential to grow. But if people repeatedly fail to deliver, that needs to be addressed and improved.

• Set realistic expectations and keep your word. It can be very challenging for a passionate and optimistic startup founder to set realistic deadlines for what they can deliver. Nevertheless, try to promise less and over-deliver. If for any reason you aren't able to hit a dead-

line, let people know well ahead of time.
- Show up with heart and passion. Act with integrity and commitment to your values.

Trust is being safe in the feeling that others will have your back when things go wrong.

The number one priority for every leader should be hiring the right people, with the right values and mentality. But that's just the first step.

In a post-pandemic world, many startup teams have a remote or distributed setup. People or whole departments work in silos, isolated from one another. That can pose a challenge to your team's resilience. Deep levels of trust are built through common experiences - and that's harder to do remotely. If people don't know each other well, you can't expect them to operate well together if things get turbulent. To compensate for the lack of spontaneous social interactions and random chats around the coffee machine, initiate rituals and practices that inspire better relationships and a collaborative spirit.

Inspire meaningful connections between employees: Leanplum

Customer engagement platform provider Leanplum[12] (Now a CleverTap company) understands the value of building meaningful connections between employees. One of their favorite programs is called "Big Talk

---

[12] *Leanplum (By Clever Tap) is an engagement platform, delivering experiences that are timely, tested, and relevant to the customer. It was founded in Silicon Valley in 2016.*

Lunches"[13]. Once a week, up to ten employees across departments go out for lunch with a stack of "big talk" questions to chat about. The questions range from "What was your first memory of success?" to "What is your biggest motivation and why?". Often, groups get so engaged that they stop using the cards as a prompt and ask their own big-talk questions. "Big talk" lunches and "Big talk" dinners get included in company retreats and other internal events. According to the co-founder of Leanplum, Momchil Kyukurchiev, such practices are crucial for establishing trust.

On top of regular operational meetings, include different activities that bond people together. It doesn't all have to be work-related. During the pandemic, Cristobal and his team at Startup Wise Guys experimented with various activities such as: "cooking together", "happy hours" and "virtual yoga classes" that helped the team connect more often.

We recently coached a startup that is operating fully remotely. They've created a weekly practice where each individual must spend 15 minutes with another person from the team, drinking a coffee "on Zoom" (during working hours). There's no agenda. They can talk about whatever they want. These meetings help the team to get to know each other and collaborate better.

Overcoming difficulties together strengthens your

---

[13] *Engineering, L. (2018, August 15). How LeanPlum builds meaningful connections with big talk lunches. Medium. https://eng.leanplum.com/how-leanplum-builds-meaningful-connections-with-big-talk-lunches-7876eec6e51*

team

In an article for Forbes[14], Tracy Brower suggests that "Going through hard times is one of the things that can create bonds between people. In fact, the more difficult the experience, the more bonding that may occur." Brower emphasizes 4 factors that fuel bonding:
- Shared experiences
- Solidarity
- Reciprocity
- Post Traumatic Growth

The article cites research conducted at the Norwegian University of Science and Technology[15] which demonstrated that going through a crisis causes the brain to release greater amounts of oxytocin. The brain chemical affects groups and relationships as it tends to make us feel good, connected, and concerned for others.

Use every opportunity to bring your people together, and create experiences in which they overcome difficulties as a team.

Team resilience-improving offsites: MailerLite[16]
Ilma Tiki, a co-founder of email marketing software

---

[14] Brower, T., PhD. (2021, April 4). Hard times make for stronger bonds and greater happiness: here's why that matters. Forbes. https://www.forbes.com/sites/tracybrower/2021/04/04/hard-times-make-for-stronger-bonds-and-greater-happiness-heres-why-that-matters/?sh=582132faf73b

[15] Grebe, N. M., Kristoffersen, A. A., Grøntvedt, T. V., Thompson, M. E., Kennair, L. E. O., & Gangestad, S. W. (2017). Oxytocin and vulnerable romantic relationships. Hormones and Behavior, 90, 64–74. https://doi.org/10.1016/j.yhbeh.2017.02.009

[16] MailerLite is an email marketing software developer that was founded in San Francisco, California in 2010. It employs people from all over the world.

developer MailerLite and author of "Leaving the Base Camp", suggests using your team offsites as a tool to improve trust and resilience.

"A crisis is a great time to find out if you're surrounded by people you can trust, but you don't need to wait for a real crisis. You can organize "uncomfortable team building". Astronaut training includes having hard experiences together - such as "uncomfortable hikes" - to learn more about each other and build trust. At MailerLite we like to organize such experiences for our team.

Once we did a hike with our team that lasted 11 hours. We split people into teams and assigned a psychologist to each group. It was a great way to learn about one another and how we act when things get challenging.

For the first couple of hours, everyone was showing up as their best self, but when exhaustion kicked in towards the end, they revealed more. While some wanted to act immediately and resolve things, others would stop, reflect, and challenge the direction. Some people chose to remain silent. We spent the whole day after the hike reflecting on the experience and the learnings with the help of the psychologists. I highly recommend you try and find ways to put your team through inconveniences and challenges. Don't wait for a major crisis to happen. Prepare your team well in advance."

3. Invest in Wellbeing & Personal Growth

According to a study by N. Mguni, N. Bacon, and J. Brown, wellbeing and resilience are positively correlated[17]. When people are taken care of and feel well - mentally, spiritually, emotionally, and physically - their capacity to face adversity is enhanced. Remember the first few months of the COVID-19 pandemic? According to the World Health Organization: "in the first year of the COVID-19 pandemic, global prevalence of anxiety and depression increased by a massive 25%... One major explanation for the increase is the unprecedented stress caused by the social isolation resulting from the pandemic. Linked to this were constraints on people's ability to work, seek support from loved ones, and en-

---

[17] *Mguni, N., Bacon, N., & Brown, J. F. (2012). The wellbeing and resilience paradox. The Young Foundation.* https://youngfoundation.org/wp-content/uploads/2012/10/The-Wellbeing-and-Resilience-Paradox.pdf

gage in their communities."[18]

We believe there's another factor, though. Let's think about it. We were locked at home. Gyms were closed and movement was restricted. Consumption of alcohol and junk food increased and overall a lot of people got out of shape. Do you think their performance improved and their stress levels decreased? To build a resilient team, you need to look for every opportunity to promote employee wellbeing.

Take a proactive role in empowering and enabling wellbeing

Imagine a culture where everyone has developed strong wellbeing habits: sleeping well, eating healthily, exercising consistently, taking sufficient breaks during the day, and having proper mental and emotional support available. Will a team like this will show up better when times get tough? You bet. In an article for Harvard Business[19] review Shawn Achor and Michelle Gielan note: "Resilience is about how you recover, not how you endure". The authors believe that "The very lack of a recovery period is dramatically holding back our collective ability to be resilient and successful."

In startups with endless to-do lists and a lot of passion from founders, the intense periods of hard work need to be balanced with proper rest and rejuvenation.

---

[18] World Health Organization: WHO. (2022, March 2). COVID-19 pandemic triggers 25% increase in prevalence of anxiety and depression worldwide. World Health Organization. https://www.who.int/news/item/02-03-2022-covid-19-pandemic-triggers-25-increase-in-prevalence-of-anxiety-and-depression-worldwide

[19] Achor, S. (2023, January 19). Resilience is about how you recharge, not how you endure. Harvard Business Review. https://hbr.org/2016/06/resilience-is-about-how-you-recharge-not-how-you-endure

Mandatory exercise to stay on top: FastTrack

Christo Popov, Founder & CEO of global consulting company Fast Track[20], and his team believe strongly in the power of wellbeing and energy (mental as well as physical)[21]. According to Christo, who was a guest on Marian Temelkov's The Leaders Who Care podcast, taking care of the energy of every team member is his number one priority and responsibility as a leader.

One of FastTrack's company values is "Die empty". That means give it your all. The working environment is competitive and ambitious and it's not for everyone. But those who are in know that this makes them stronger and more resilient as a team. *"You only grow as a human being if you experience difficulties,"* Christo noted.

He sets rules to accomplish this. One of them is: *"In our company, everybody has to go to the gym during office hours. Going to the gym [on a daily basis] is part of your job".* The company has a gym and if you want to work for FastTrack you have to spend one hour there every day. This helps keep everyone healthy and prepared mentally and physically for the work they need to do. *"If you have more energy in the body [and] in the mind you will be able to do [what you want to do] better and enjoy it more,"* concluded Christo.

That doesn't mean we recommend this exact prac-

---

[20] *Fast Track is a global consulting company, founded in London, UK in 2012.*

[21] *Temelkov, M. (2023, March 03). Celebrating Bulgaria Liberation day With Christo Popov: TLWC Episode #105. The Leaders Who Care. YouTube.* https://www.youtube.com/watch?v=vjGWmJYeHWY

tice to every startup team. You do you!

Consider what you can do within the context of your own values and philosophies.

Maybe you start a #wellbeing Slack channel where everyone shares daily updates. Or you commit to cover employees' membership for gym and yoga classes. Or if you work from an office you ensure there are always fruits and healthy snacks available.

What practices can you develop that inspire and improve employees' wellbeing?

Learning is another ingredient that will make your team stronger. Investing in the learning and personal development of your employees will not only contribute to better retention and motivation, it will make you better equipped for difficult times. The most forward-thinking companies allocate resources to upskill and grow their employees. That can come in different shapes and forms, for example: investing in courses, training programs, or coaching, allocating "company time" for activities related to learning and personal development. LinkedIn's first CHRO, Steve Cadigan, believes every company should have a core commitment to learning in today's changing times. During his four-year tenure, starting in 2009, LinkedIn grew from 400 to almost 4000 employees. In the early days, the company wasn't able to compete with the other tech giants on salaries and benefits, so they focused on providing learning & growth opportunities.

"You have to build learning into the job," says Steve. "And that's a part of the compensation we should be talking about with people... That was our competitive advantage at LinkedIn." Team members were able to learn through challenge and responsibility. "Putting people in situations where they are going to learn new things and are given more responsibilities than others would give them, unlocks enormous energy," Steve adds.

People who constantly learn and grow are better prepared to face challenges and resolve problems in a crisis. They are also more likely to stick around when things get tough. After all, you invested in and cared for them. This will make them more motivated to help resolve any problems.

People, especially A-players, often really want to get coaching from their manager with feedback and input on a weekly basis. This grows their skills and builds a history of success, enabling them to be promoted. As Steve Cadigan says: "Don't wait for the learning department to have a learning class on whatever. You need to give [your employees] new projects, new experiences, new assignments, and new rotations. It's on you as leaders. And that's part of the "growth thing". You have to design an experience that's going to add value to the company and add value to them."

What can you do to empower learning and personal development?

Personal development hour: Stoyan & his team

Stoyan and his team have a weekly ritual called "personal development hour". Every week, the team spends 60 to 90 minutes together, during company time, discussing a topic related to personal development. The topics are not necessarily focused on role-specific needs but range more widely. Examples of themes are: developing personal habits, time management, networking tips, personal branding, journaling methods, nutrition strategies, or how to provide and receive feedback. Team members volunteer to prepare and moderate the sessions. In some cases, the team brings in an external expert. The sessions help people expand their horizons and contribute to higher engagement, motivation, and an increased sense of belonging.

"You have to invest in the learning and development of your team," Stoyan says. *"Personal development hour has become a team favorite. Since we started, I can see increased commitment and motivation from everyone; with real dedication when we encounter those hurdles that sometimes inevitably occur. The team is increasingly proactive, taking ownership and having each other's backs.*

For example, recently I had a cold a few days before an important corporate training session I was delivering. There was still a lot to prepare and the client requested last-minute changes. New content and materials had to be developed. My team took the initiative, showed up, and had my back. They worked overtime and helped prepare everything. The training ended up being a success despite the hiccups and I knew I had a team I could rely on."

4. Create Clear Structures & Processes

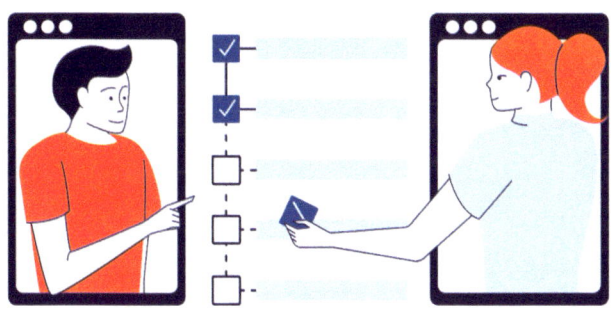

A crisis may disrupt you and your operational efficiency, but you will be a lot better prepared to face one if you have well-established structures and processes. Startups often struggle to create effective structures and processes. Early on it doesn't seem like good use of time. Execution and creating momentum are what matters: You build your product, identify your target market, start building the core team, and focus on finding a product-market fit. Once you start growing, you need to make the leap from "hustle culture" towards a more "structured culture" (aka "systematic culture"). This will help in uncertain and difficult times, because:
- It will save you time and energy, allowing you to move faster
- You can be more agile when shifting roles and responsibilities
- It will improve productivity and efficiency
- It can reduce the risk of making mistakes when times get stressful

Processes that are important to set in place include:

- **Organizational Structure**

    The organizational chart. Be explicit and have a shared understanding of everyone's roles and responsibilities and their level of decision-making.

- **Team Management**

    How is the team managed? How do you set goals and objectives? How often do you have team meetings, what is the agenda, and who chairs them?

- **Talent Attraction & onboarding**

    How do you acquire new team members? What kind of employment package do you offer (responsibilities and compensation in a broad sense). What are the specific requirements and expectations for each employee? How do you keep them accountable? What is your onboarding process?

- **Sales processes**

    What is your step-by-step process for generating leads and acquiring customers? Who do you target and how do you measure progress? What CRM system (and other tools) do you use?

- **Legal & contracts**

    Creating legally approved contract templates to use with employees, customers, and other stakeholders.

- **Accounting**

    Setting up the procedure of who does it, when it is done, and what tools to use. Creating guidelines for what counts as a company expense.

- **Product Development**
  What processes do you use to build your product? Do you operate in sprints or use Kanban? How do you figure out what to build and how do you build it efficiently? Who is responsible for each part of each process?

- **Budgeting & finance**
  How do you budget and estimate cash flows? Who makes decisions about fundraising and spending?

Processes to stay on top of your finances: SlideHub

SlideHub[22] is a Denmark-based company that helps professionals manage and access their best practice presentations and slide assets. They have been serving a growing number of advisory businesses and B2B organizations across the globe since 2016.

"Our approach at SlideHub is that we never leave things to chance," explains Anders Thomsen, co-founder and CEO. "Instead, we follow processes to ensure our finances are out of danger. These processes follow 3 principles:

1. Have a cash flow forecasting model
   We have created a model that estimates the most

---
[22] *SlideHub is trusted by over 500 companies due to their on-demand PowerPoint design service and implementation support.*

probable amount we will have in our account 1 to 30 days from today. Keep it simple. We are using Excel. The model calculates income vs expenses. It includes data on the amounts we expect to receive from each of our clients (or other funding), and expected exact payment dates, based on the average time it took them to pay us in the past. It also includes our expenses and the exact day we need to pay them. Having this model keeps us in control. At a glance, we have an overview of our cash flow forecast. We can easily do scenario planning and predict how decreasing certain costs will affect our liquidity. This short-term forecast can be complemented by longer-term scenarios.

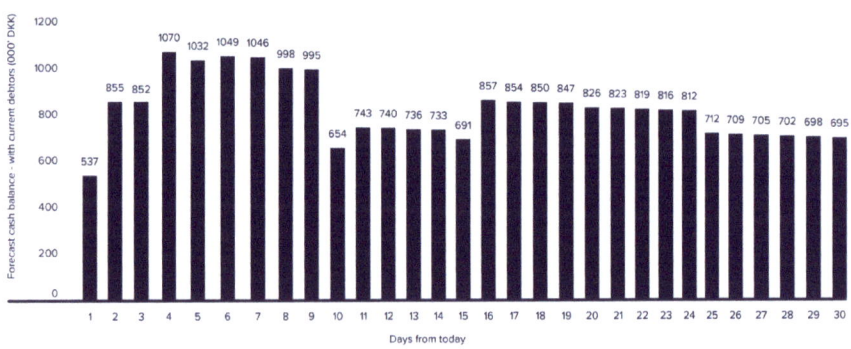

Set clear terms and chase outstanding invoices

You need to chase outstanding invoices in the same way you chase clients for sales, especially if you are operating B2B like us. At SlideHub we negotiate terms with each client. Our default payment terms are 15 days from invoicing. If a client prefers longer payment terms, we might allow it, but we increase the price. Corporations will often offer payment terms: 30 days or 60 days, and there might still be delays. As a startup, do not accept such terms. Negotiate them. We are very meticulous about invoice payments, and you should be, too. If a client is ever late on a payment we contact them right away and request the payment to be made - of course in a respectful manner. But you need to be liquid and have good working capital.

2. Act fast and secure your finances

In a crisis, you need to act fast. One of the good things about having sound processes in place is that it allows you to make decisions fast. But don't be fooled, processes in themselves won't make you more resilient. They need to be smart and agile.

When COVID-19 hit, we quickly understood we would be financially affected. Back in 2020, our offering was primarily on-demand PowerPoint solutions for businesses. When the pandemic hit in 2020, the demand for our services dropped almost immediately by 40%. Our clients didn't need PowerPoint support. Everyone was cutting costs and freezing budgets. We started burning DKK 250,000 per month instead of 50,000 DKK, as we did in the two months prior. Instead of being on our way to profitability, our runway dropped down to 5 months.

We knew we had to take action right away to secure healthy finances. We came together and started looking for ways to improve our cash flow. We organized not one, but two board meetings in March 2020.

Here are some of the concrete measures we took within the first two weeks of the crisis hitting:

- Cost reduction measures
  - Decreased founder salaries by 40%
  - Negotiated a 20% salary cut with employees
  - Pushed VAT, Tax Payments, and Social Security whenever possible
  - Offered subcontractors long-term contracts (saving us costs on a yearly basis)
  - Sent home 3 salespeople for 3 months, securing 75% of their salary from the state. (No outbound activity made sense anyway)
  - Tried to renegotiate short-term rent

- Revenue/ cash-boosting initiatives
  - Reached out to clients to request payments on pending invoices
  - Wrote emails to all former and current clients to remind them we are open 24/7
  - Innovated with new, simple offerings such as credit packages
  - Reached out to existing Pay-as-you-go customers to sell credits at a discount (we needed the cash)
  - Moved people from our operations/delivery team to Customer Success and reached out personally to all existing clients (aimed at increasing volume)

- Funding initiatives
  - Secured a EUR 50,000 loan (in case we needed more cash)

- Requested a few more loans
- Applied for funds from a few innovation programs and state funds
- Talked to our bank for a potential credit line extension
- Researched state-supported loans

Fast forward to 2024: we not only survived the crisis but came out stronger. Triggered by the crisis, we've built a SaaS platform to support the on-demand design business and currently, we employ 45+ professionals across offices in Denmark, Portugal, and Mexico. Our revenues have grown 3x since the beginning of 2020 and the team is more resilient than ever."

5. Embrace Adaptability & Resourcefulness

Adaptability is the capability of an enterprise to react quickly to opportunities and risks and convert them into business advantage (Macmillan & Tampoe,

2000)[23]. In a resilient culture, a team can adapt quickly to the changing environment, shifting resources and direction. Agility and structure are not mutually exclusive. Sound processes can provide a good foundation and allow you to act fast, as SlideHub did. It's easier to change your plan when you had one in the first place.

This concept is fundamental in the book "The Hard Thing about Hard Things"[24]. The author, Ben Horowitz, distinguishes a Peacetime CEO from a Wartime CEO. He argues that successful leaders must be able to adapt to different contexts and leadership styles depending on the challenges they face. "Peacetime CEO knows that proper protocol leads to winning. Wartime CEO violates protocol in order to win."

Being adaptable means you might have to bend the rules. A crisis of any nature will bring complexities that you might have never been faced with before.

Finding new opportunities to work your assets and resources: Dimo's Pizza

When the COVID-19 pandemic unfolded, Chicago pizza place Dimo's Pizza suddenly lost a big chunk of its sales. Dimo's made 70% of its revenue from selling pizza slices and was not equipped for home delivery[25]. Like many small businesses, the restrictions put in place due to the pandemic put the company in difficul-

---

[23] Macmillan, Hugh; Tampoe, Mahen (2000). Strategic Management. Process, Content and Implementation. Oxford University Press Inc. New York.

[24] "The Hard Thing about Hard Things" is a business book written by Ben Horowitz and published in 2014.

[25] Lussenhop, B. J. (2020, April 10). Coronavirus: I'm using my pizza oven to toss masks for nurses. BBC. https://www.bbc.com/news/world-us-canada-52232381

ties.

Instead of despairing, they acted and adapted to the circumstances. It turned out pizza ovens burn much hotter than regular ovens, which means they can bend industrial-grade plastic. Dimo's started using sheets of industrial-grade plastic to make face shields for healthcare workers. *"We do have these ovens that are quite useful,"* Dimitri Syrkin-Nikolau told the Chicago Sun-Times at the time[26]. *"If we can find another way to put them to use, they're going to help people, especially in this tough time."* The team at Dimo's Pizza got busy. They launched a crowdfunding campaign and donated thousands of face shields and pizzas to frontline healthcare workers.

Instead of asking the question: "How can we sell pizza?" they asked, "How can we utilize our resources to generate value for the marketplace and for our community?". Tara Kline, who had worked at Dimo's for more than five years, told the newspaper that adaptability felt good. *"It built me up a little bit to realize that even if we're in the midst of a massive pandemic, you can turn your pizza shop into a successful PPE production area,"* she said. That decision helped Dimo's Pizza get closer to its community and come out of the crisis even stronger.

In resilient cultures, team members are resourceful.

---

[26] Lee, M. (2020, November 8). *Dimo's Pizza uses ovens to make coronavirus face shields - Chicago Sun-Times. Chicago Sun-Times.* https://chicago.suntimes.com/business/2020/11/5/21540810/chicago-coronavirus-ppe-dimos-pizza-face-shields-personal-protective-equipment

Sometimes the solution is not obvious. You need to find it and be open to the unexpected. We used to call this mindset 'thinking out of the box' before the term became overused.

In an article for Shopify[27], Braveen Kumar shares learnings from dozens of entrepreneurs, each of whom had at least one story about being stuck. "Building a business is like navigating a maze without a map," he writes. "And every once in a while, you're bound to hit a wall. Knowing how to be resourceful in these difficult situations and finding creative ways around challenges is what sets successful entrepreneurs apart."

The article notes 5 ways to be more resourceful:
1. Pause, zoom out, and find your north star
2. Get good at Googling (problems are rarely unique)
3. Find inspiration in your competition
4. Don't be afraid to ask for help
5. Consider pivoting your business

To inspire a resourceful and adaptable culture, empower creativity and innovation throughout your team. Set up brainstorming sessions. Let your team come up with ideas - wait until the end to share yours. It's tempting to say something "can't be done" and "let's move on" when an idea is only half-baked. That can turn people off and destroy your team's innovation spirit, making them more afraid to take ownership and come up with solutions when a real crisis hits: the learning is that if they get it wrong, they might get punished. In a resil-

---

[27] *Resourcefulness in business: a critical skill for success. (2022, April 10). Shopify.* *https://www.shopify.com/blog/resourcefulness*

ient culture, everyone can step up and take ownership when it's needed.

When we asked Ilma Tiki, cofounder of MailerLite what makes a resilient team, she answered:

"Diversity". A diverse team can see a problem from a variety of angles. Diverse in any sense of the word: people from various geographical backgrounds, skill sets, and ages, with different passions, interests, and characters, introverts and extroverts.

6. Lead with Decisiveness & Courage

Decisiveness can be defined as "the ability to make decisions quickly and confidently"[28]. In a crisis, both you and your team need to be decisive. To cultivate such leadership qualities across the organization, a

---

[28] *Decisiveness. (2024).* https://dictionary.cambridge.org/dictionary/english/decisiveness

founder needs to let go of control and let team members take more ownership. When a team member asks what to do or how to do something, we often feel the urge to respond by telling them how. It will save us time immediately, so we can move on faster. But if we always take control and define the solution, we cripple our team. That's not to say you should never answer such questions. You are the leader and you are expected to be in charge. However, leaders can gain from letting people figure out the solution themselves.

Incorporating coaching practices into your leadership can have a positive effect. Coaching is about guiding the other person to find clarity and answers themselves. Instead of saying "We should do X", ask more often: "What do you think we should do?", even when the answer is clear to you. This approach inspires critical thinking. Once the employee starts working on the task, they will be more engaged and committed to delivering. After all, it was their idea: they will do their best to make it a success.

Unless you are in a critical situation, you should let your team make mistakes, even if you can see that they might not be taking the optimal direction. Letting your employees experiment, make decisions themselves, and allow them to fail in a low-stakes environment improves their confidence and sense of ownership.

"I actually like it when my employees make mistakes. Because when you make a mistake it means you are actually risking something. You are trying to go further and beyond what you know. You are taking a risky path to achieve something better."
- Victor Sanchez, Co-founder & CTO, SkillMapper[29]

In many startups, employees are afraid to take initiative and make decisions. Crippled by fear, they worry about making the wrong decision. When a real crisis happens, stress and panic get added to the equation, and people freeze: They don't have the ability to respond.

Leaders need to equip team members with decision-making skills and responsibilities. One of the tools we recommended in our previous book is the RACI matrix. (Responsible, Accountable, Consulted, Informed). It's a great tool to help a team clarify each person's roles and responsibilities, and, very importantly, how decision-making is distributed.

In one of the very first PERFORM workshops we held with a group of startups, we asked them to create a full RACI matrix. After completing the exercise, one of the founders was shocked to realize how much of the decision-making fell to him. He was 'accountable', 'responsible', or at the least 'consulted' for the majority of the company workflow. During the workshop, he commit-

---

[29] *SkillMapper is a startup, building the future for search and discovery in e-learning. SkillMapper was founded in Paris, France in 2020.*

ted to making changes and becoming better at delegating.

Can you relate? Do you have to make your organizational chart clearer and give your team more authority?

A few years ago, Cristobal had to make some adjustments himself. When he had a small team, it was natural that most decisions went through him. The team at minimum consulted with him before moving on. As the Startup Wise Guys team grew, this was no longer efficient. During the annual company offsite, Cristobal brought up the topic. He drew a picture with himself in the middle and arrows pointing at him, representing the decisions that went through him. Then he drew another picture of how he imagined things should be in the future. He didn't have to be part of every decision anymore. It was time for the team to grow.

Today each department operates a lot more independently. Cristobal was strict in adhering to the new system. When asked about something, not in his 'department', he would refer it to the person accountable. This has worked tremendously well for everyone. The team gained confidence and capability. When the company faced challenges, the whole organization was far better able to face them.

In a crisis, you need warriors. People who are capable and ready to come together as a team, to move fast and boldly, and not be afraid of what they are facing. Remove any signs of "analysis paralysis". Momchil Kyurukchiev, co-founder of Leanplum (A Clever Tap Company) calls such team members "fighters and soldiers". According to Momchil, it's very difficult to have a resilient culture if people don't possess this mentality individually. In fact, to this day it is a checkbox he needs to tick before approving someone new to join the team. "In your startup, you need people who are hungry, people who never quit. You can not hire people solely on their skills and CV. They have to be fighters as well, so when things get tough you can rely on them." says Momchil.

Act in line with your values - even more so in a crisis

As a startup, you are in it for the long run. Your actions in difficult times will dictate the direction of your culture for the future. Do you have to ensure your company survives? Absolutely. But under pressure, it can often be tempting to cut corners and make decisions that will bite you in the long run. Upholding your values is more important when your company struggles than at any other time. Use them as a compass for how to act.

It's all about the people: Startup Wise Guys
At Startup Wise Guys, we had finally gone through the worst of the COVID-19 pandemic. We managed to keep the promise to our employees that nobody would be fired due to our finances. We were feeling settled... and then the Ukraine war hit.

At the time we had 41 Ukrainian portfolio companies and three of our managers were Ukrainian. Our entire team wanted to help, asking what our policy was for this and whether they could take time off to cope or help.

Cristobal called a team meeting. The Ukrainian managers were reassured: *"Take whatever time you need to help your people. When you feel you can get back to work, let us know, we have your back".* He told the rest of the team: *"If you feel you need to take time to help Ukraine and the initiatives to support the Ukrainian people, take off the time you need, no questions asked".* But there was also a message to those who stayed put: *"Don't feel that you are not helping because you are still working. We are going to take care of the company so our colleagues can take care of themselves."*

In the coming days and weeks, half of the team was involved in support projects. Almost overnight, they built a database of information to link incoming requests for logistics, business, or humanitarian help with people who could offer assistance. Later on, many in the team said they were shocked and didn't see any purpose in their work during the early days of the war. Being able to put their energy and time into humanitarian projects made much more sense. They felt the company had empathy for the reality of their situation.

This policy of course had an impact: We had fewer resources and lost some projects. But so what? The team knew the company cared, for the long term. The policy aligned with the purpose and values and did not focus on short-term needs.

Your values should serve as a compass for how you make decisions. Sticking to them will help you in a crisis.

Building a resilient (startup) culture

Leaping through a crisis: Cosmic Centaurs

In Q4 of 2021, 18 months into Cosmic Centaurs' existence, the team received the most incredible news. Both Marilyn Zakhour, CEO and Founder and Tala Odeh, the first person to join the company and one of its most senior members, were pregnant. They were even due to give birth within weeks of each other. Obviously, it was delightful news - but Cosmic Centaurs were a team of only six people. Two out of three senior team members, accountable for more than two-thirds of the revenue, would be away for a few months. It could become a crisis for the nascent business.

"The centaurs doubled down on what we believe sit at our core: our purpose, our values, and our commitment to one another," explains Marilyn. *"From day one, our purpose was to make work better, not just for our clients, but also for the centaurs themselves. Our values of Community, Compassion, Curiosity, Creativity, Excellence, and Discipline serve as guiding principles that we refer to on a daily basis and in all of our interactions.*

Our Values
Our values sit at the core of who we are

Curiosity
We google a lot, we ask a ton of questions and we question everything.

Compassion
We go the extra mile to make people feel appreciated, heard and involved.

Community
We know it takes a village, that's why we spend time growing and nurturing our network.

Creativity
Creating is at the core of what we do. We believe in our own creativity and the creativity of others.

Discipline
We believe that discipline will set us free. We are committed, diligent, and hard working.

Excellence
We never settle for average. We believe in adding value in everything we do.

This moment in our company's story was no different. Marie Nakhle, the third-most-senior leader on the team, jumped in to lead the organization without hesitation, making sure that our work, rhythm, and outputs would not be impacted."

The three juniors on the team took on more responsibility too, sometimes owning entire work streams that had so far been managed by one of the leaders.

Throughout this time, Marilyn and Tala were never made to feel like they were letting the team down. Quite the opposite, it was all done with positivity and care and in line with the values. For example, the team organized wonderful online sessions (baby showers and welcome back parents sessions) to celebrate the milestones with Marilyn and Tala, allowing them to share their experiences as moms-to-be and new moms.

"Both the lead-up to this important milestone and the return to work were handled efficiently and in line with the company's values. When the new moms returned, the team started work on building an even more scalable and sustainable company. They doubled down on client acquisition, effective delivery, and sustainable growth, activating their values of creativity, excellence, and discipline." This allowed us to create a strong pipeline off of the back of increased visibility and reputation for our brand and work," notes Marilyn.

The company now employs nine people and more than doubled its revenue in 2023.

Key takeaways

• Focus on creating a culture that nurtures your team. As a starting point, make sure you and your core team align around your Purpose, Vision, and Values.

• Take care of your people in good times. Then they will be more likely to show up and fight together with you when times get tough.

• Rituals and practices make a real difference. Cultivate rituals that fuel a resilient culture.

• Implement the Resilient Culture Manifesto to help your organization thrive when times get tough:
   1. Inspire Optimism
   2. Build Trust & Collaborative Spirit
   3. Invest in Wellbeing & Personal Growth
   4. Create Clear Structures & Processes
   5. Embrace Adaptability & Resourcefulness
   6. Lead with Decisiveness & Courage

• Act in line with your values, even in the hardest times. It will define who you are as a leader.

Opportunity Story

From crisis to reinvention: Handplayed

Angel Ivanov is the co-founder of Handplayed[30], a creative production company headquartered in Sofia, Bulgaria.

"In 2018, we were lucky enough to be trusted in the local Bulgarian market. We were a young video production company working with the major advertising agencies and their multinational clients, producing several projects per month. Our revenues were growing and our team was riding the wave.

This all came to a grinding halt in 2019, when our main partners, the agencies, started integrating vertically to offer video production services to their clients directly. It was a move we had anticipated, but it still caught us off guard. We lost 50-60% of our revenues. Towards the end of the year, our team was uncertain about the future of the company. It coincided with the first mentions of 'Covid' in the news.

We sat down and opened a presentation we hadn't updated for a while: the one with our values, mission, and vision. It clearly stated that we are in this business because we are passionate about creating high-quality audio-visual work. But something else stood out that we could now assess from a new perspective: We cared about what was being said in our films, as much as we cared about how well it was said.

---

[30] *Handplayed is a full-service content creation studio, based in Sofia, Bulgaria.*

Being producers working for agencies, we didn't have much say about what the ads were communicating. We were there to turn compelling creative into memorable films. If we were to survive without the agencies, we'd need to work with clients directly. That meant we had to write the scripts and turn them into videos. We had to reinvent the way we do business.

So, we scratched out the antiquated 'video production' label and became a content creation studio. We were still experts in production, but we started internal training in creative development, reorganized our production team, and hired our first creatives. Clients could come to us with or without an idea in mind. We'd work with them on everything from creative research and strategy to producing the finest pieces of content.

Currently, our team is evenly distributed between creative and production. We all pride ourselves on the independence we gained through this transformation and the passion and quality of our work. Thanks to the transformation our team grew 6x and the revenue 5x compared to 2019. Facing a crisis forced us to revisit our business model and come out stronger."

CHAPTER 2
Planning & effective crisis response

In this chapter:

Building strong organizational habits

Predicting a crisis: noticing risks and preparing to face them
- Doing a pre-mortem
- Developing a crisis management plan
- Crisis management and business continuity

Effective crisis response
- Minimizing the damage
- Adjusting your planning rhythm
- A crisis requires difficult choices

The 4 areas to always keep top of mind
- Team, Clients, Cash, Brand

"Don't wait until you're in a crisis to come up with a crisis plan."
- *Phil McGraw, American television personality and author*

Planning & effective crisis response

For an organization to be productive, the leadership team needs to master *planning* and *execution*. Planning can be defined as "setting the company goals, and determining a course of action for achieving them". Execution is "carrying out a plan".

They go hand in hand:
- Insufficient planning, even with solid execution might mean you waste time and resources on what shouldn't be done at all
- Insufficient execution, even with solid planning might mean missing out on producing results and achieving desired progress

In our first book[1], we explored a number of tools and methodologies that the most effective teams use to manage their workload and produce results. We also discussed what gets in the way of your "Focus & Exe-

---

[1] *"PERFORM: The Unsexy Truth about (Startup) Success"* was published in 2020. It includes practical strategies and examples to help you craft your company culture.

cution": the 5 villains of focus and execution and how to minimize their impact.

In this chapter, we will explore how to best prepare for a crisis, what to prioritize when it hits, and how to respond to it effectively.

Building strong organizational habits

If you are a leader or a manager in a company, pause here. Which of the two elements is your team currently doing better: Planning or Execution? Which one do you need to pay more attention to and improve?

Don't wait for a crisis to happen to start building strong organizational habits. Start today. Assess how you and your team are currently doing and see if there's any space for improvement now.

Exercise: Planning & Execution

How well are you doing? Ask your team to anonymously grade themselves and to grade the team from 1 to 10 in each of the four areas. For example:

	Planning	Execution
Individual performance	8	6
Team performance	6	7

Take the average scores and have a discussion with your team about what you can do to improve.

Often as leaders, we are blind to the obstacles that prevent the team from doing their job well. These can be wide-ranging - from unclear priorities and unclear roles to insufficient communication about what is happening in the company.

When asked about her main task as a leader, Kate Williams, CEO at 1% for the Planet[2] said: *"I feel like the most important thing that I can do is to create the conditions for every person in my team to be wildly successful at their jobs."*

Prioritize making time for regular strategy meetings. Discuss your goals and objectives frequently. Make sure both team priorities and individual responsibilities are clear to everyone. Test, try, improve, and find a system that works. As Andrew Tarvin, author of "Humor that Works[3]", suggests: *"The best system is the one that you use".* [4]

To ensure the purpose of tools and meetings is clear to everyone, capture them in a sheet like this:

---

[2] *1% for the Planet is a global organization that inspires businesses and individuals to support environmental nonprofits through membership and everyday actions. Started in 2002 in Burlington, Vermont.*

[3] *Tarvin, A. (2019). Humor That Works: The Missing Skill for Success and Happiness at Work.*

[4] *Source: Yankov, S. (May 2020). Humour as a Productivity Tool: Coffee & Productivity #5 with Andrew Tarvin. Productivity Mastery. Spotify.* https://open.spotify.com/episode/5PTxE0uvc7feJDluMCMrFL

Meeting type	Frequency	Duration	Who is involved	What we discuss (Agenda items)	Who organises it
Strategic	Quarterly	Full day	The whole team together	Strategic overview, Evaluate quarterly progress, Define quarterly OKRs, Discuss strategic company important topics, Team building and alignment	John
Check ins	Weekly	One hour	Everyone (in teams)	Weekly achievements, what was not achieved and why, learnings and opportunities	The John of each department
Stand-ups	Daily	15 minutes	Everyone (in teams)	Share updates, Measure progress, Define daily objectives	The John of each department
Planning method	OKRs, Sprints	Tools we use	Notion, MIRO, ClickUp		

Predicting a crisis: noticing risks and preparing to face them

" If you don't choose to do it in leadership time up front, you do it in crisis management time down the road."
- Stephen Covey, Management consultant and author of The Seven Habits of Highly Effective People

A crisis cannot always be predicted, but an effective leader should always stay alert and be ready to face one. Part of the time you allocate for planning and strategy should include risk management analysis to predict potential risks.

Keeping track of risks: RemoteMore

RemoteMore[5] is a Chicago-headquartered company that helps developers find full-time remote jobs. Its CEO and co-founder Boris Krastev takes risk management seriously.

"Risk management is very important to me. It should be very important for every startup. I invest a significant amount of time thinking about the risks and classifying them. On my computer, I have a menu bar shortcut to my Risk Analysis sheet. It currently has 65 risks. I like the idea of knowing what's unknown and what the issues are. I don't like to be surprised by things that I could have anticipated. And even though we can't predict every-

---

[5] *RemoteMore is a company that gives equal access to job opportunities to everyone, regardless of where they are based. It was launched in 2019 in Copenhagen, Denmark.*

thing, you'd be surprised how often we are actually able to foresee the biggest risks.

I also use this to align myself with my team. For example, I often ask my co-founders and management to share the risks and challenges they see ahead. Essentially, every risk & challenge is an opportunity we can exploit to improve our company. Every 60-90 days we meet and go through the list, discussing what can hit us and what to do to avoid it. Having these risk management sessions helps us to be best prepared for whatever challenges lay ahead of us."

Identify the key areas that might involve risks for your company. Stay alert and update yourself constantly on global trends, industry news and technology developments. Pay attention to internal and external risks and act quickly to mitigate them.

Preparing for the worst: Vivino

Heini Zachariassen is the founder and former CEO of Vivino[6]: the largest wine app in the world with over 61 million users. One of the main revenue channels for Vivino is charging its sellers a marketing fee for every bottle of wine sold through the platform.

In February 2020, Heini and his co-founders were closely watching the spread of COVID-19. *"We didn't*

---

[6] *Vivino empowers people to enjoy wine to the fullest by using crowd-sourced data to personalize wine recommendations. As the world's largest online wine marketplace and most downloaded wine app, their community is made up of millions of wine drinkers from around the world, coming together to make buying the right wine simple, straightforward, and fun. Vivino was founded in 2010 in San Francisco, USA.*

know what was going to happen. We didn't know whether all our sales would disappear...As soon as we saw this coming, we started pushing the brakes. No hiring, no marketing and we cut the costs all the way down," explains Heini. The team started anticipating what could go wrong. One of the questions Heini likes to ponder is: *"What is the worst thing that can happen?".* In this specific case, the answer was that distributors would not be able to ship. If they couldn't deliver, Vivino could be in trouble. In fact, for a short time in Italy and Hong Kong, deliveries were shut down.

Heini didn't leave things to chance. He called the product team to explore how quickly they could build a product for wine pickups. He talked to his legal department in the US to try and get a sense of the situation and the alternatives they had. *"I always like to work on different options. Do we have a Plan B and a Plan C? It also helps you mentally to talk about those things at least."*

Heini and the Vivino team prepared as much as they could for the upcoming crisis.

In the end, everything worked out fine. There were no major delivery disruptions. Moreover, the pandemic meant people were at home and alcohol deliveries increased. Vivino's revenues grew in 2020. In business terms, the year was successful for Vivino.

Reflecting on the situation, Heini says he would do the same again: make sure the company is best prepared to face a potential crisis, even if in the end it doesn't occur.

Exercise: A premortem

A great exercise to identify the risks that can lead to a crisis is to run a premortem.

A premortem prepares for the worst by assuming the company has already failed at a certain point in the future. The thought experiment aims to identify the risks, threats, and potential failure points that would have the biggest impact on the company - and of course to brainstorm solutions to prevent them. You can do the exercise yourself, but to make it more effective, invite your co-founders, management team and/or some of your team members to join in.

1. Set the session framework
- Make sure everyone is clear on the objective of the exercise
- Set the framework, using a question such as: "Imagine 6 months from now our company has failed. What crisis or challenge put us out of business?"

2. Brainstorm potential risks
- Jointly brainstorm up to 50 failure points
- Invite people to think of various types of risks: Legal, Internal team, Brand/PR, financial, industry-related, global trends, etc.
- Collect all answers on a flipchart or a MIRO board and sort them into categories.

3. Identify Top 10 failure points
- Go through all risks and rate them from 1 to 10 in terms of:
  - Probability
  - Impact Level
- Multiply these two factors and identify the top 10 failure points.

4. Brainstorm risk-mitigating solutions
- Brainstorm ideas, strategies, and solutions for minimizing or entirely preventing the risk for each of the highest-scoring failure points.

5. Commit to concrete next steps
- Assess the proposed ideas and solutions. Discuss them with your team.
- Commit to concrete actions. Prioritize these and assign responsibility for each task.

Planning & effective crisis response

Developing a crisis management plan

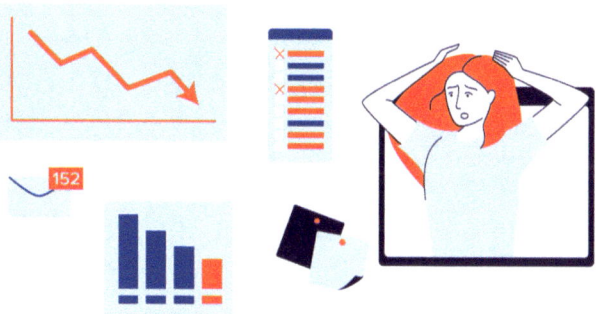

Identifying the risks is only part of the equation. You also want to create a concrete plan of action: a crisis management plan. What will you do as a team if a specific crisis or situation occurs? Who will be focused on resolving the crisis? Who will ensure business operations run while the crisis is ongoing (business continuity[7] plan)?

Make sure to keep in mind both crisis management and business continuity. Discuss different scenarios together with your team and agree on how you would address the situation if it occurs. When you are preparing the plan, keep in mind that you might have to change it faster than normal if a crisis does hit.

Let's have a look at the team of BotsCrew[8], a Ukrainian company that creates custom chatbots and

---

[7] *Business continuity may be defined as "the capability of an organization to continue the delivery of products or services at pre-defined acceptable levels following a disruptive incident".*
https://en.wikipedia.org/wiki/Business_continuity_planning

[8] *Since 2016 BotsCrew has been named top chatbot development company by Clutch in 2017 & 2018, with clients that include startups that raised 10m now*

voice assistants, and how they prepared and handled the Russian invasion. Nazar Hembara, CEO & Founder, tells the story.

Crisis management & business continuity plans: BotsCrew

"On 24 February 2022, Russia invaded Ukraine in a major escalation of the war Russia began in 2014. In the weeks before, it was clear that an escalation was very likely. However, nobody in the team expected the scale of this new terrible wave of war. However, we started discussing the risk and our actions in January. First conversation started with the top management team. We discussed the risks and our potential actions. The next step was an update to our Business Continuity Plan with immediate action items.

In early February, we held an all-hands meeting with the whole company. We openly told them about our concerns and the risks, with a plan for what we would do. We offered help with relocation for our employees and their families in the East of Ukraine and declared support for the families of our colleagues who would join the military. I was the one letting everyone know. It was crucial not to underestimate the risks, while at the same time not demotivate everyone by scaring them.

The message was: "Risks are high; we don't know what will happen, but we are prepared, and we will do our best to support our team and our country as much as we can." I emphasized the positive things like our cash balance and reliable long-term clients who had expressed their support. Our management team repeat-

edly communicated that the safety of the team and their families would be the highest priority. The management team had also prepared a good Business Continuity plan for each department and sub-team.

We had a lot of conversations with clients. 90% of our clients are based in the US, UK, or Western Europe, and it was crucial to communicate our plan. We've outlined all the key areas and shared them with the clients. Personal touch and relationships were essential to maintain trust in us and our plans. Clients were highly supportive but quite worried. Constant communication on all levels, not just from top management, was crucial.

Being prepared helped a lot. I would have loved it to be one of the plans we have never needed. But in the early morning of the 24th of February, the management team knew what to do and acted without hesitation.

The priority was to bring everyone to safety. It was a logistic and emotional nightmare, but given our preparation, it was manageable. The best thing about having a plan is that you don't have time to panic. You act on your plan. That's it. A person with a plan feels much more reassured and confident and can act wisely in extreme situations, even if it's no longer possible to carry out the plan as it was.

We donated 1.3 million Hryvnia ($50,000) to the Ukrainian army two days before the full-scale escalation. Everyone felt an urgent need to do something - the war was coming. It was a moment that united us and showed that we share the same values.

I admire how our team acted in the first days. It was an example of autonomy and unity in highly challenging times. One of our colleagues joined the military on the day of the invasion.

Our priorities were clear:
1. Take care of your safety.
2. Work if you can.
3. 100% of the money we make as the team goes towards salaries and donations to the Ukrainian army.

We announced our intention to donate all profits to Ukrainian resilience immediately.

After getting themselves and their family into safety, everyone in the team kept working. It was clear to everyone that we had to, in order to retain our clients and be able to support our country and families.

It worked well and helped all of us get through this challenging year. Business, personal and national priorities were all one and the same.

As a result, thanks to our fantastic team, we:
- Were joined by a new teammate less than a week after the invasion
- Retained 100% of our clients. Thank you!
- Grew by 36% as a business in 2022
- Got 16 new clients, including some of the world's largest companies like Honda and Adidas
- Recruited 17 new teammates in 2022

But most importantly, we had the honor of helping the Ukrainian Forces defend Ukraine. In total, we've donated roughly $250,000 in goods like radios, helmets, bulletproof vests, ambulances, SUVs, etc.

What advice can I give to fellow founders in tough environments?

Planning & effective crisis response

> 1. *Build a great team and trust them to do their work*
> 2. *Have a plan*
> 3. *Communicate openly with the team about the challenge and the plan to overcome it*
> 4. *Be true to yourself and your values"*

Effective crisis response

While preparation is key, some crises will inevitably hit no matter how much you prepare. Sometimes they will come as a surprise.

This is what happened to Metafy[9], a company that helps gamers monetize their talent. One morning in March 2023, the team woke up to realize their bank, Silicon Valley bank, was on the brink of bankruptcy.

Below is an unfiltered LinkedIn post by the COO of Metafy - Victor Folmann, from March 13, 2023, one day into the crisis.

---

[9] *Metafy is a company, founded in New York in 2020, that enables gamers to monetize their talent through 1:1 live coaching, courses and content.*

9 steps to face an unexpected crisis[10]: Victor Folmann, COO at Metafy

"I haven't slept for the past 24hrs. Sorry for any typos.

In times of crisis, it's essential to take action to safeguard your business. At Metafy, we've been impacted by the collapse of SVB, and we're taking proactive steps to ensure our company remains operational.

Fortunately, we had a cash reserve at another provider.

Here are nine steps I've personally executed in the past 24 hours to increase the likelihood of successfully weathering the storm.

1. Consulted with experienced individuals who have navigated similar situations in the past.

2. Suspended all recurring non-essential software services and removed credit card information to avoid unexpected charges.

3. Initiated negotiations with all creditors to delay upcoming invoices by three months.

4. Diversified our cash positions across all merchant services.

5. Scheduled eight meetings with debt providers for next week.

6. Opened a new bank account with another provider and diversified our limited cash reserves.

7. Communicated transparently with our team to in-

---

[10] *Folmann, V. (2023, March 11). Source: https://www.linkedin.com/posts/victor-folmann_i-havent-slept-for-the-past-24hrs-sorry-activity-7040389772342689792-OD1Z?utm_source=share&utm_medium=member_desktop*

form everyone about our plans and actions.

8. Updated all merchant services to ensure that incoming funds go directly to our accounts during this time of uncertainty.

9. Consulted with shareholders and learned sentiments on supporting us with additional funding.

As entrepreneurs, we know that tough times make us stronger. We remain committed to overcoming this challenge and sharing our experiences with the community. Let's stay resilient together."

A few months later Victor shared his reflections on the experience with us:

"Metafy got through the crisis. We survived this terrible period and emerged from it with a more robust financial plan. This was realized through our critical measures during those 72 hours.

After that, we perfected our banking arrangements by using numerous vendors but still kept the credit line open with SVB. This crisis has shown us how important it is for us to intentionally design the safety of our finances and leverage such opportunities for better conditions across all banking services.

If there's one piece of advice I could give to my fellow founders and operators, it would be about the need for preparedness as well as flexibility. Always make sure you have alternatives in case of anything because you should never depend on only one financial institution alone.

Diversifying your banking relationships and regularly reviewing your financial strategies can provide critical safety nets in times of unexpected financial turbulence."

Planning & effective crisis response

Minimizing the damage

When a crisis hits it's important to act fast and put out the biggest fires. As Victor Folmann noted, the first few hours are crucial. This is also usually the time with the most uncertainty and moving parts. Dust yourself off and try to understand the situation as well as possible. If you can, find a few minutes to "cool your head" and get ready to lead.

And then, just like Victor Folmann, quickly identify how to minimize the potential damage. Bring your team together as quickly as possible. Discuss the situation and create a checklist featuring everything that needs to be addressed immediately.

We call it *a list of fires*. Think of "fire" as everything that is already "burning" and has the chance to grow fast in potential negative impact. Before you address anything else, you need to focus all your resources on putting out the fire.

The SSS framework: XploraBG

Georgi Malchev, founder & managing partner at XploraBG[11] recommends a simple framework you can come to that will quickly set your mind to focus on what matters. *"In a crisis when things get tense, it's easy to lose perspective and get into a reactive mode, which is often not the most constructive way to deal with a situation. Instead, I prefer to do my best to regain control. The SSS framework helps me with that."* shares Georgi.

---

[11] *XploraBG is a digital agency, headquartered in Sofia, Bulgaria, with a human-centric approach to advertising, branding and marketing.*

Planning & effective crisis response

Situation

Once the big fires are put out, gain clarity about the situation. What caused the crisis to happen? What further consequences and developments can you expect? What resources do you have at your disposal to deal with the situation?

Strategy

Once you calmly assess the situation, you need to create a strategy. What are your most important goals in front of you? How would you allocate your resources to address the crisis most effectively? Who would you make responsible for delivering on each of your goals? What should you keep in mind for the plan to work?

Steps Ahead

What are the most important next steps for you and your team? What specific actions should you laser-focus on and in what sequence? If necessary, make a checklist and organize it in order of priority. Then go out and execute.

In day-to-day business, your planning cycles might be longer-term. In a crisis, you have to accelerate the frequency of planning, prioritization, and team alignment, because updates, progress, and crisis development can have a direct impact on where the team should focus.

Planning & effective crisis response

Adjusting your Planning Rhythm: The Startup Chat

In a podcast interview from 2020[12], Steli Efti (Founder at Close.com) and his co-host Hiten Shah (Co-founder & CEO at Nira) discussed how they change their planning mindset in a crisis. Both believe planning timelines shrink. When the pandemic hit, Hiten initially increased the frequency of planning to hour-by-hour. A few weeks later, when there was more clarity, he would plan on a day-by-day basis and sometime after, week-by-week. Steli's quarterly and monthly planning cycles went down to weekly. That way he would have a better chance of adjusting and adapting fast. He recommends avoiding rigidity in forecasting: making 3 or 6-month plans could end up being a futile exercise to "try and control the future and make things safe". If you plan too far out, it's easy to get attached to that story and stick to it, instead of adapting to changes in the context or situation.

The crisis response wheel

Make sure you create pitstops for you and your team to observe how the situation evolves and make adjustments if needed.

---

[12] *Source: The Startup Chat podcast, episode #517 with Steli Efti and Hiten Shah (2020, June)* https://thestartupchat.com/ep517/

Planning & effective crisis response

The crisis response wheel typically has four stages:

1. New information

Seek out updates on how the crisis is developing as well as the results of measures you have taken. Make sure you distinguish facts from rumors. Keep in mind that not every new piece of information will be relevant. Filter it accordingly. In its 2019 Global Crisis survey[13], PwC notes: "In crisis, getting facts quickly and basing your response on them, are key to successful outcomes. In a world of split-second virality, incorrect, insufficient, or misleading information (or even correct information spread at the wrong time or in the wrong way) can increase your exposure and amplify the crisis." When managing a crisis, you are dealing with probabilities, so any new information may affect how you decide to act. Things will often change very quickly, so you need to stay alert.

---

[13] *Source: PwC. (2019). PwC's Global Crisis Survey 2019. PwC.* https://www.pwc.com/ee/et/publications/pub/pwc-global-crisis-survey-2019.pdf

2. Updating the plan

While you assess the new information, discuss whether your plan needs any adjustments. Are there any new "fires" you need to put out that you haven't thought of before? Is every person on the team doing well or do you need to shift responsibilities among them? Make a decision on how to proceed.

3. Team alignment

Communicate clearly and align with your team. Make sure everyone knows what's expected from them. In stressful times, communication may be more difficult. Use alignment meetings to hear people out as well. Let everyone speak up about their feelings and anxieties. Share motivation and support. Get everyone on the same page.

4. Execution

Get everyone focused on the task at hand. Stay focused and get things done. Continuously gather information and stay alert about how the crisis evolves. Be ready to shift and switch the plan and priorities depending on how the situation develops.

Depending on the type of crisis you face, the frequency might differ. In certain cases, you might have to go through the crisis response wheel several times a day.

A crisis requires difficult choices

Being a leader comes at a cost, especially in a crisis. Jon Gordon, leadership author, consultant, and speaker, noted in a viral post on X (formerly Twitter): *"Everyone wants to be a leader, but very few want to lead"*.

As a leader, you will be tested. You will be required to make decisions. Sometimes you will not have enough information to make an effective choice, but you still have to decide and lead. In an evolving crisis, every minute of indecision can be costly.

> "In any moment of decision, the best thing you can do is the right thing, the next best thing is the wrong thing, and the worst thing you can do is nothing."
> - *Theodore Roosevelt, U.S. President*

You need to make decisions and often you will have to do it fast. In some cases, none of the options will seem good and you will have to make the 'least bad' choice. It will feel horrible and you might have doubts. This will be the time to go back to your values and trust your intuition.

Making hard choices in times of crisis: Winston Churchill

1940 - the Second World War. Hitler is winning in Europe and the future is bleak. The English and French forces are pushed back towards the coastline in France by an advancing Nazi army. A miracle is needed for the more than 338,000 British and French soldiers not to be captured or killed: it could mean defeat. The stakes are high and the tensions are rising. UK Prime Minister Winston Churchill is running out of time. American

President Theodore Roosevelt refuses to send any official American vehicles on a rescue mission. Churchill decides to act on the famous "Operation Dynamo", involving thousands of civilian boats and ships on a mission to save the soldiers. Some 4,000 Allied soldiers are assigned to strongly resist the Nazi onslaught in an attempt to slow it down while the evacuation is ongoing. However, there's no evacuation planned for them. Churchill makes the incredibly difficult choice to sacrifice 4,000 people. This leads to over 338,00 soldiers being saved. Four years later Nazi Germany was defeated. That night, according to several accounts, Churchill told his top military advisor General Hastings Ismay that he *"felt physically sick."* [14] Despite that, he did what he had to do. Difficult times require difficult choices.

The 4 areas to always keep top of mind

Regardless of the type of crisis, there are 4 areas to constantly keep in mind and take care of: Team, Clients, Cash, and Brand.

team   clients   cash   brand

---

[14] *Source: Gilbert, M. (2014). Churchill: A Life. Rosetta Books.*

Planning & effective crisis response

1. Team

Your team is the backbone of your organization. Their safety and well-being should be a top priority in a crisis. A crisis can create a stressful and uncertain environment, and it is essential to provide your team with the support they need to navigate the situation successfully. Before a crisis hits, try to investigate what would most affect your team.

Questions to explore with your management team when a crisis looms:
- How can you best look after your team?
- Do we have the right team and skills to face what's coming?
- Do we have to change the way we work - shift priorities and responsibilities among us?
- Will there be any delays in salaries or other hiccups that need to be communicated?
- What are potential stress factors and how can we minimize them?
- Do we need to hire a coach or psychologist to support our team?
- What additional support might be needed?

2. Clients

It's important to investigate how a looming crisis may affect your clients and do your best to be there for them. This involves providing support as well as securing existing and upcoming deals.

Questions to explore with your management team:

- Which of our clients may be affected by the upcoming crisis and how?
- What pains/challenges are our clients most likely to experience?
- What services/products might become "nice-to-have" and removed from our clients' budgets?
- What new products and services can we create that will be valuable to our clients now?
- What can we do to support our clients through the crisis beyond this - to show we care and build goodwill?
- How do we ensure smooth and frequent communication with our clients during the crisis?

3. Cash

Crises can lead to unpredicted expenses and disturbed cash flows. Be extra careful about your cash and liquidity.

Questions to explore with your management team:
- Do we have stable cash flows in the months to come?
- Do we have to minimize our costs? For how long? What can we do to cut costs?
- Are there possible payment delays from clients we should be aware of?
- What can we do to close deals faster and receive payments upfront?
- Will any furloughs or layoffs be required? What will that mean? How can they be optimized and communicated most effectively?
- Are any of our clients likely to have difficulties and budget cuts? Who should we prioritize talking to?

- If we need funding: what can we do if funding stalls?

4. Brand

It's also important to check how the crisis can affect the company's brand/reputation.

Questions to explore with your management team:
- Can the crisis lead to PR/brand damage?
- Can the crisis affect the reputation of our industry, and with it, our brand?
- Will the crisis response actions affect our brand reputation?
- How do we prevent sensitive information from leaking and causing a brand crisis?
- How can we strengthen our brand/reputation in times of uncertainty?

Key takeaways

• Review your organizational habits of planning and execution. Find a system that works for you and your team and keep improving it.

• Prepare well for a potential crisis by frequently estimating risks that can affect your business. Use exercises such as "premortem" to identify threats and address them in good time.

• If a crisis is likely, take the time to prepare a crisis management plan. No crisis will unravel exactly as you pre-planned, but a solid plan will help you focus on what matters most, especially in the early days of the crisis.

• Once a crisis hits, keep calm and identify "the biggest fires". Put them out first. Adjust your planning rhythm with more frequent cycles. Take on new information, adapt your plan accordingly, and get everyone on board for a new phase of execution.

• During the course of the crisis, make sure the 4 areas are taken care of: team, clients, cash, and brand.

Opportunity Story

Thinking out of the box and responding effectively to COVID-19: Grand Hotel Kempinski Vilnius

April, 2020. Kai Schukowski is alone in the Grand Hotel Kempinski Vilnius. Kai was the youngest ever appointed general manager in the history of the Kempinski Hotels chain. Usually very cheerful and positive, this evening he is not in a great mood.

"I remember sitting alone in an empty lobby - the hotel was closed for a few weeks. It was sad, and I didn't exactly inspire positivity. It was tough for everyone, but eventually, I thought to myself: 'I can either drown in self-pity or I can do something about it.'

I went back to my usual exercise habits and started rebuilding my positive mindset. Fish smells from the head. If I'm negative and depressed and let that rub off on my team, that's probably not going to help. Instead, I decided to focus on what was within my control. I realized that after reading the news, I felt down. Once I stopped paying attention to it, I could feel the change in my energy.

If you focus on what you can control and on inspiring positivity, you start seeing opportunities in the crisis. I started organizing meetings on Google Meet with my team, so everyone could pitch ideas about what we could do to improve our situation. To be honest, there were a lot of rubbish ideas. But that's the point. When you have nowhere else to go, any idea is something worth talking about. Then someone said: "Why not turn our rooms into restaurants?".

It was a great idea. We removed the furniture from all the rooms and turned all individual rooms into individual restaurants. It allowed us to operate our restaurant when all the other places to eat in the city were closed. It was such a brilliant move. We had so many reservations, and people are still asking if they can do it again. This idea literally kept us afloat financially, because we didn't have any income at all. It obviously generated less income than what we would normally make and we had to reduce the team. But this idea alone was crucial for the continuation of our business - and it came out of one of these whiteboard jamming sessions where somebody proposed it and we went with it.

I think it's super important to get your team onboard - just because you're the leader you don't need to have all the answers. If you adopt a positive mindset towards crises and problems, you naturally find the opportunity. It will deliver more than spending time plotting every possible scenario - you'll still be shocked if one comes true. Instead, prime yourself with positivity to be ready and deal with things as they happen."

CHAPTER 3

Mastering crisis communication

In this chapter:

7 ways to increase communication effectiveness in a crisis
- Transparency & Vulnerability: (Re)gain Trust
- Empathy: Listening and Understanding
- Frequency: Embrace the power of over-communicating
- Alignment: Share a consistent message from all team leaders and stakeholders
- Be Action-oriented: Plan for different scenarios
- Expand your reach: Leverage multiple channels and formats
- Learn & Adapt: Use data to understand the effectiveness of crisis communications

PR and External Crisis Communication
- External Crisis Communication: How do you prepare?

"Clear communication during turbulent times is a beacon of hope."
- *Anonymous*

As we mentioned in our first PERFORM book, robust communication equals communication that is effective, authentic, and pervasive. It is robust, defined as strong, and unlikely to fail. Communication is a two-way process of reaching mutual understanding. Participants not only exchange information, news, ideas, and feelings but also create and share meaning. As such, communication should connect, engage, and be consistent, creative, and meaningful. It is, however, a huge challenge for time-poor CEOs. Many underestimate the importance of internal communication in their day-to-day activities. This is never more true than in a crisis when demands on leaders' time intensify, while the need to communicate well (both internally and externally) also ramps up.

Founders and leaders often test different ways of communicating effectively while growing and scaling. When facing a crisis, even more efficiency is needed. Communication is an essential leadership tool in turbulent times, but a crisis brings day-to-day communication challenges, such as:

- How do you ensure important information reaches everyone?
- How do you create a safe environment, where ideas and feedback can be shared freely when the situation is very uncertain?
- Which channels and communication rituals best fit the company culture in a crisis?

Many founders only develop communication skills when they need them. They learn to speak in public to pitch during the growth phase and develop some written skills to communicate with investors. It's also common to see founders and even CEOs outsourcing this expertise internally, or externally, by hiring ghostwriters. While everything is going well, this can be OK: a good CMO can "speak outward," a good CHRO can "speak inward," and things "work." However, in a crisis, the involvement of founders and the CEO often becomes essential, and that's the worst time to discover that you ought to have invested in developing these skills.

Many new variables also come into play and must be addressed in a crisis, such as lack of trust, personal financial uncertainty, redundancies, and psychological safety[1]. Your team will be stressed. This will add to the challenging task of getting the message across to all levels of the organization and to other stakeholders, to motivate them to move together towards new short- and mid-term objectives.

In this chapter, you will learn about the elements that ensure you communicate effectively and robustly in a crisis. In emergencies, you have to tackle both internal and external factors.

7 essential elements of robust communication in a crisis

- Planning, Bi-directional communication, Alignment, and Frequency, the four pillars of robust communi-

---

[1] "The belief that the work environment is safe for interpersonal risk taking." Source: Edmondson, A. C. (2019). The Fearless Organization. John Wiley & Sons.

cation from our original book, evolve and get supercharged during a crisis. The tense and stressful environment a crisis creates requires more. We've added the essential features of Transparency & Vulnerability, Expand your Reach, and Learn & Adapt. In a crisis, Transparency & Vulnerability - encapsulated in your approach and attitude to communication - are so fundamental we've put this as number one.

This gives us 7 essential elements of robust communication in a crisis:
1. Transparency & Vulnerability: (Re)gain trust
2. Empathy: Listening and understanding
3. Frequency: Embrace the power of over-communicating
4. Alignment: Share a consistent message from all team leaders and stakeholders
5. Be Action-Oriented: Plan for different scenarios
6. Expand your Reach: Leverage multiple channels and formats
7. Learn & Adapt: Use data to understand the effectiveness of crisis communications

1. Transparency & Vulnerability: (Re)gain Trust

"What we call basic truths are simply the ones we discover after all the others[2]".
- *Albert Camus[3], French philosopher and author.*

Transparency

As leaders, we expect our employees and stakeholders to trust us. In a crisis, skepticism sets in, alongside stress and uncertainty. Many will regard you as the person who led the company into a difficult situation, or at the very least wasn't ready when the crisis hit. Regaining trust is fundamental. It all starts with transparency.

In startups, everyone knows a bit of everything. Avoid fuelling drama and gossip by sharing what's re-

---

[2] The line continues: "... However that may be, after prolonged research on myself, I brought out the fundamental duplicity of the human being. Then I realized, as a result of delving in my memory, that modesty helped me to shine, humility to conquer, and virtue to oppress. I used to wage war by peaceful means and eventually used to achieve, through disinterested means, everything I desired." Source: Camus, A. (1991). The fall. Vintage.

[3] Albert Camus was a French philosopher, author, dramatist, journalist, world federalist, and political activist. He was the recipient of the 1957 Nobel Prize in Literature at the age of 44, the second-youngest in history.

ally happening. The leader's task is to give the facts in a narrative that helps the company throughout the crisis. Keeping team members informed helps build trust and a sense of ownership among team members. This in turn drives engagement and commitment to the company's success.

You need to be as open and honest as possible with your team, even about topics that can be uncomfortable to discuss, such as the company's financial situation, potential risks, or challenges that may impact growth. Some information can't be disclosed, but leaders should strive to be as transparent as possible about the situation, its impact, and the steps being taken. When there's something you can't share, make sure your team knows this and be honest about the potential impact of these 'hidden' details. This is a very powerful engagement tool and often leads to people being more committed to overcoming challenges.

Last but not least: Be reliable. It's essential to deliver on your commitments no matter what. This helps leadership teams to (re)build trust one step at a time.

Showing transparency and clear direction when executing difficult decisions: Fractory

Martin Vares is the CEO of Fractory[4], the Estonian industry 4.0 startup revolutionizing laser cutting. The startup is thriving, but as a consequence of the war in

---

[4] *Fractory is a B2B Industry 4.0 startup focusing on laser cutting manufacturing, ounded in 2017. Originally from Estonia, it has 3 co-founders. with headquarters in Manchester, England. At the end of 2022, the company had 67 employees and nearly €2 million in revenues. It is seen by many as a potential future Estonian unicorn.*

Ukraine and the global macroeconomic conditions, Martin made the tough decision to close the US business in 2022. It was paramount to communicate the decision with transparency to rally the company around. Let's hear Martin tell the story:

"It was unpleasant, upsetting even. But it came down to pure math. The cost of successfully entering [the U.S.] is significant, but it became insurmountable when the cost of borrowing rose so steeply. We needed to clearly communicate this to the team.

I wanted Fractory to continue to grow. It was going to be touch-and-go financially to become profitable in the US. We just did not have the cash. In the Nordics and the UK, we could do it, so it was wiser to focus there, instead of risking everything to break into an expensive market.

It was vital to clearly and transparently communicate that peril: to continue was to risk everything. This was conveyed in company-wide communications and in the personal conversations we had with everyone. We wanted it to be understood that we had looked at every scenario and every expense, with the goal that Fractory would come through the crunch ahead and still be there thriving and providing a quality service.

The team at Fractory responded with understanding and respect towards the difficult decisions made during a challenging period. They appreciated the honesty and transparency shown by the leadership, which fostered a mature atmosphere. The clear communication about the factors driving the decision helped everyone grasp the necessity of prioritizing growth in a more stable and familiar market. This collective understanding reinforced the sense of unity and commitment to the company's goals."

Martin stresses the importance of being open and sharing: *"When you have to make a decision on your own, it's super important to loop everyone in afterward. Just share your reasons clearly so everyone gets why you went the way you did. It keeps things transparent and builds trust, even though you decided to go solo."* He suggests involving others in decisions whenever possible: *"When you can bring others into the decision-making process, it really helps to get different points of view on the table,"* he notes. *"This not only makes things more transparent but also shows you're open to hearing what others think. It's a great way to make everyone feel included and respected. In both cases, just being clear about how you got to your decision—whether it was all you or a group effort—really shows your willingness to be open and vulnerable. It helps everyone understand and trust the process a lot more."* Rebuilding trust, he notes, takes more than words: *"Actions matter most... you need to show that you're genuinely committed to the principles you've set out."*

For Fractory, the open communication paid dividends: *"Fractory became more efficient and doubled down in the markets where we already had large customer bases. That was the goal and the message. It became a self-fulfilling prophecy as the team rallied around and made the leaner model work."*

> *"Vulnerability is not winning or losing; it's having the courage to show up and be seen when we have no control over the outcome. Vulnerability is not weakness; it's our greatest measure of courage."*
> *- Brené Brown, professor at the University of Houston[5]*

Vulnerability

We often have an image of startup CEOs as superheroes. We may even see ourselves as one. But even superheroes make mistakes. In fact, in most movies, the story builds around the superheroes' mistakes and moments of self-doubt. Own up to the fact that the company is in a crisis for a reason and openly explain to your team that you made mistakes along the way. Be vulnerable. It shows honesty. By letting your guard down, you demonstrate trust in others, which encourages others to trust in turn.

As CEO of Startup Wise Guys, Cristobal has personally faced this scenario on several occasions. It's tempting to "just" explain the plan. But it's important to first explain the mistakes and what led to the situation - as well as why those decisions were made at the time. Make sure that although mistakes were made, the team understands the thought process that led to those decisions. "I want them to see that I am vulnerable, as well

---

[5] Brené Brown is a research professor at the University of Houston, holding the Huffington Endowed Chair, and a visiting Professor in Management at the University of Texas and a best-selling author." Source: Edge, C. (2023, April 20). Great Leaders Show Vulnerability: Why it is a Leadership Strength!. Corporate Edge. https://corporate-edge.com.au/great-leaders-show-vulnerability-why-it-is-a-leadership-strength/

as re-establish trust because we will be making difficult decisions going forward," notes Cristobal.

Displaying vulnerability can be a powerful communication tool for fostering empathy, building trust, and deepening relationships. It makes it easier for employees to relate to you as a leader. Everyone is likely to be feeling weak, unsure, or vulnerable in a crisis. Seeing a leader express those same feelings creates a sense of connection. Playing your part in expanding the sense of belonging is crucial to keep the team united.

When a leader or an influential individual shows vulnerability, it also sets the tone for a safe and open environment. It signals to others that it's okay to be human, to make mistakes, and to have weaknesses. It breaks hierarchies by reducing the distance between leadership and team, eliminating "us versus them", and fostering and encouraging collaboration. It builds a safe environment in which people can start sharing how they feel and their ideas on how to solve problems. This way, more brains will be working on the issues and the crisis becomes easier to face.

2. Empathy: Listening and understanding

People process crises differently. Having empathy involves understanding those differences. Addressing the concerns and fears of your stakeholders is important, but your team must come first: it is your most valuable asset and the foundation of your culture. Communication needs to be multidirectional, but without losing focus on what is truly strategic. That's the real challenge.

Don't expect everyone to perform at 100%, especially soon after the news has hit the floor. Allow time for meetings that are not operational, where people get a chance to share their concerns and fears, and where you actively listen. By listening to and understanding the feelings of others, we develop empathy and compassion. That connection is what helps the team see the crisis as "our problem" rather than "the company's problem."

Approaching communication with humanity, empathy, and compassion will mean answering two fundamental questions from employees. First: "Will I be fired?". Employees will want to know how the crisis impacts their safety and job security. Secondly, they'll want to understand any impact on how they work and what they value in the company - including their colleagues.

To respond, use words and phrases that show your concern, appreciation, and solidarity. For example: "We understand how difficult this situation is for you" or "We appreciate your patience and cooperation". These messages must be delivered sincerely - just saying the words isn't enough. The team needs to feel genuine empathy and compassion in every action, every word, and every move from the company and the founders.

"The word teaches, the example moves"
- Portuguese saying.

This requires you to actively listen and pay attention to what people say and how they say it. Acknowledge their views and feelings. You need to dedicate time to this. Even if you're ready to move to action, your team may need days or even weeks to process the news and the new situation.

Importantly, you need to respond to your team and their feedback. Never assume that the answers are already known. Establish a clear mechanism for acting on feedback and communicating changes back to the workforce. This will not only improve communication but also help (re)build trust. An employee needs to understand that they've been heard and that what was said has been assessed, even if it doesn't result in action. If this doesn't happen, it can be as detrimental as not listening at all, creating a sense of deception and undermining connection.

Use every informal opportunity you have to personally collect one-to-one feedback and get a variety of views. Every time you have a call with a manager or an employee, ask them how they are feeling and how they are doing. Check to make sure people understand the important information you communicate.

Ensure managers and team leads at all levels help disseminate information and address concerns within their teams. Encourage more junior leaders to share their team's concerns with the senior leadership. Look after junior leaders as they're more "likely to break". The trust and personal bonds created, facilitate an environment where everyone can speak up to share concerns and questions.

Meanwhile, pay attention to the fact that as a leader, your manner and attitude can set the tone for the entire organization. Whether you are ready to acknowledge it or not, you will be stressed in a crisis. Even when you're stressed, it's crucial to project a sense of calm, control, and optimism in your communication. Add this to your transparency and realism. The team needs to believe that you will lead them out of this crisis.

3. Frequency: Embrace the power of over-communicating

Frequency relates to how often you communicate with other team members. A Quantum Workplace[6] study carried out in 2022 notes that the frequency of one-on-one meetings strengthens the connection between a manager and employee, and the employee's connection to their work - they'll mitigate challenges better, narrow the skills gap, and understand growth opportunities. Employees are most likely to want to meet with their managers on a weekly basis[7].

These frequencies correlate with a feeling of engagement (see Barchart.) The engagement will spur employees to give their all every day and care about the success of the business.

---

[6] *Paulsen, E. (2022, July 13). The Best One-on-One Meeting Frequency According to Research. Quantum Workplace. https://www.quantumworkplace.com/future-of-work/one-on-one-meeting-frequency*

[7] *36% want to meet weekly, compared to 27% monthly, 11% quarterly, 5% 2-3x a year, 5% annually or never and 17% when needed; Source: As above.*

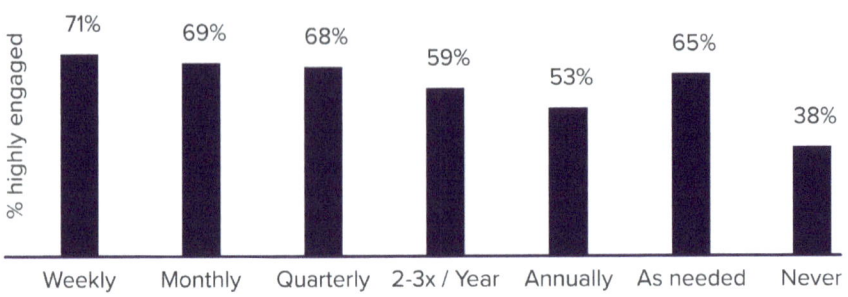

In normal times, you need to check in with your team at least once a week. In uncertain times, it is important to over-communicate. Regular updates, even if there's not much new information, help alleviate anxiety and keep everyone aligned. A lot of research[8] and evidence shows that people with elevated stress levels are more likely to experience a decline in cognitive function, affecting their capacity to remember, concentrate, and learn new things. This makes regular updates paramount when times are uncertain.

From the CEO/leader's point of view, silence may mean that everything is the same as in previous days or weeks. Your employees, meanwhile, are more likely to believe there is no good news or that things are worse than expected. Silence can also bring doubts

---

[8] *Kulshreshtha, A., Alonso, Á., McClure, L. A., Hajjar, I., Manly, J. J., & Judd, S. E. (2023). Association of stress with cognitive function among older black and white US adults. JAMA Network Open, 6(3), e231860.* https://doi.org/10.1001/jamanetworkopen.2023.1860 *See also chapter 5.*

that generate distortions and parallel stories, leading to disengagement and an escalation of the crisis. A crisis doesn't tolerate information vacuums. Those most interested in resolving the issues must take charge of the narrative and the information flow.

Updates should always be regular and planned, so the team knows when they will be shared. Effectiveness works in a similar way to advertising, where the recipe is relatively simple: reach x frequency. If we take this concept into internal communication in a crisis, we start with a defined 'first segment' of influential people. Just as in an ad campaign, they will become your 'digital ambassadors' as long as the content is good and engages them. Continuing the advertising analogy, you can then expect them to spread the message 4x more successfully[9,10] than the company-wide announcements you make (if we see the latter as equivalent to traditional media). This is because friends sharing the message brings 88%[11] more credibility, according to ad-industry data.

Startups evolve over time. The evolution is not always linear and will often include some kind of crisis. "Business puberty," the time when a startup has scaled to reach a certain size, is one of these critical

---

[9] *Internal results from a project with Brazilian e-commerce brand Netshoes (6 months tracking): Nano-influencers (influencers to a smaller audience - eg 1,000-10,000 followers) were 3.89 times more effective in converting new business than traditional media.*

[10] *Cunningham, P. (2024, January 12). 88% of consumers trust word of mouth - Buyapowa. Buyapowa.* https://www.buyapowa.com/blog/88-of-consumers-trust-word-of-mouth

[11] *Wells, S. (2024, January 17). Word of mouth statistics and key insights for 2024. Roster.* https://www.getroster.com/blog/word-of-mouth-statistics

watersheds. The dynamic of solving problems "by the water cooler" isn't working anymore. Other processes may also be past their sell-by date as the company has grown. Companies often don't change until they reach a crisis point. As a startup grows in size, however, the need for more effective internal communication increases, too.

The value of repetition in communication: JeffApp

Toms Niparts is the co-founder and CEO of JeffApp[12] – the financial superstore for Asia's unbanked, headquartered in Riga, Latvia. Let's hear from Toms about how frequent and repetitive communication was key to reverting to growth as the company scaled up and passed its puberty stage.

"We started experiencing standstill or slow speed in some areas when our company transformed from a team of less than 10 people where 'everyone fits in one room, knows everything, does everything' into a larger organization.

Initially, we thought this was normal. More people had joined. It took time for new talent with different opinions to get on the same page and learn how to cooperate.

We introduced OKRs and spent quite some time polishing them, but the results were still underwhelming. Then the revelation came: we are no longer a bunch of

---

[12] *JeffApp was founded in 2019. JeffApp accurately measures creditworthiness using alternative data. This unlocks financial services for the underbanked across Southeast Asia, where a very large proportion of the population is unable to get a bank account. Today, JeffApp has 35+ employees and has served more than 1.5 Million people in Southeast Asia.*

people in a "garage". It is not enough to give a quick intro to high-level vision, mission, and strategy when onboarding and expect alignment and speed.

We gathered half the staff and did a lot of work on "reinventing the strategy". The result was 90% the same as before, but with far better buy-in since people had been involved in developing it. Most importantly, we adopted an approach where I repeated key items related to vision, mission, and strategy on a regular basis - almost like a parrot.

Initially, it caused pushback among the company's veterans and some of the core people, but it contributed to the greater good. With a repetitive, borderline-annoying approach, OKRs, KPIs, and targets became meaningful. People could connect the tasks they carried out to the greater purpose and make sense of what they were doing.

Through this experience, I personally learned an important lesson: As CEO, you have to be borderline annoying, repeating messages way more often than you think you should. What you take for granted as being important is only one of the thousand things your team hears on a weekly basis. Consistent repetition from the CEO ensures that the core messages are strong signals, not noise."

Toms' message can't be emphasized enough. If you aren't thoroughly bored with your own message, then it is not getting through. A key trap for intelligent people is to get bored easily, and thus shift the message too soon and/or make it too complex when what's needed is simplicity. Times of crisis are riddled with uncertainty. When stressed, people will focus on parts of your message and interpret messages through their own biases. Communicate clearly and thoroughly.

You may choose to:
- Send short follow-up emails to ensure what you said is what was understood
- Summarize things in bullet points (ideally no more than four)
- Ask for 'next steps' to always be repeated before a meeting is closed
- Speak slower, use fewer words, and focus only on what's most important

4. Alignment: Share a consistent message from all team leaders and stakeholders

> **"You've got to get everyone making one movie, instead of everyone making their own movies"**[13]
> *- Shane Hurlbut, Hollywood Cinematographer* [14]

In a crisis, it's easy for a message to be misinterpreted. Discrepancies or inconsistencies in communication can also rapidly erode trust. This makes it crucial that only one message goes out. There will be internal discussions about which direction to take, but once a decision is reached, co-founders and leadership teams must be aligned. They may have different styles of communication, but the message has to be the same.

Stakeholders[15] need to be able to trust that they know everything they need to know. There are different stakeholder groups, so the one-story-fits-all approach does not work. However, although the depth and type of information disclosed to each group of stakeholders may vary, the overall message needs to be the same - consistent, transparent, and communicated to the different target groups in a form that works for each of them.

---

[13] *Source: Productivity Mastery Podcast with Stoyan Yankov; Episode #5 with Shane Hurlbut (September, 2021):* https://open.spotify.com/episode/5Bwi94D-6MQ2Qyzech8qn0T?si=dd516da26050486a

[14] *Shane Hurlbut, ASC is a Director of Photography, with more than 3 decades of experience, working on major productions such as "Terminator Salvation", "Need for Speed" and Netflix's "Rim of the World".* (https://www.shanehurlbutasc.com).

[15] *A simple and comprehensive list of stakeholders should include investors and shareholders, board members, employees, key suppliers, customers, key media outlets, journalists, influencers, government agencies.*

Mastering crisis communication

Key suppliers and customers[16] are on the list of key audiences that should be included in a strategic communications plan. This may surprise you, but an organization's reputation can suffer long-term damage if it is seen as handling a crisis poorly. This can affect all your relationships. A consistent message demonstrates that the organization is in control and is managing the situation responsibly.

Consistency does not mean all audiences receive the information at the same time. Plan the way you roll out communications to reach different audiences in the right strategic order and with as little opportunity as possible for the message to 'leak' between different groups.

If you know a media story is breaking that will be worrying employees, send them a message the night before and/or an explanatory note designed to mitigate against concerns. Adopt a similar proactive approach when you know in advance that an important customer will churn or a key employee leave. Craft a good, clear story, explaining why things are happening and what the company plans to do to move forward. Communicate individually with key people in the company and prepare to share with all employees shortly after. Keep listening to your team to ensure your communication is appropriate and tactfully deployed.

Well-crafted communication still won't stop rumors and speculation. These will always exist in a crisis. As

---

[16] *Shirbhayye, C. (2020, May 9). Supply chain crisis management – Importance of communication. SOURCING AND SUPPLY CHAIN. https://sourcingandsupply-chain.com/supply-chain-crisis-management-importance-of-communication/*

CEO, be prepared for this. Address it with care. Don't point fingers at or punish people who spread rumors. Act with empathy and understanding.

5. Be Action-oriented: plan for different scenarios

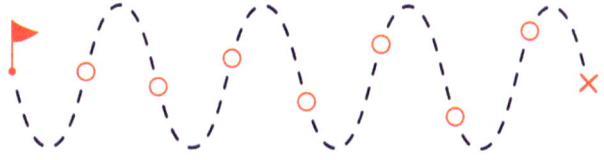

Communication must be coupled with decisive action. Outline clear steps that are being taken to address the crisis and communicate them effectively. As a leadership team, set not only big objectives but also include the smaller ones that allow you to communicate wins as they happen. Align the objectives with the team to enable them to perform well. Agreeing on the destination helps everyone run in the right direction. But while that destination is the big objective - 'the prize' - there will be hurdles along the way. Recognise and appreciate the effort and progress you are collectively making.

Always expect the unexpected: Have communication plans for various scenarios. This can help you respond more swiftly if and when circumstances change. Foreseeing potential challenges and having contingency plans in place can provide a sense of control.

How you can use powerful 90-day plans

As a norm, we recommend shorter and finite timebound plans. 90-day plans provide a useful crisis communication framework, especially when the nature of the crisis requires a phased and sustained response over an extended period. If a crisis you're facing requires a shorter timeline, adopt the framework accordingly. This type of plan provides a clear roadmap for managing the crisis and can help ensure that communication efforts remain consistent, timely, and effective.

Here's why and how a 90-day plan works well for crisis communication:

- Structure: It provides a clear timeline, helping to break down tasks and communication efforts into manageable steps.
- Phased approach: It allows you to address immediate needs first (days 1-30), followed by a middle-term plan (days 31-60) and a longer-term approach (days 61-90). This phased approach can be vital when dealing with evolving crises that have different needs at each stage.
- Planned Execution Reviews: Review and assess the effectiveness of communication strategies at each 30-day point and adjust accordingly for the next phase.
- Adaptability: The use of 30-day segments allows for adjustments based on new information or changing circumstances. You may define several potential scenarios. Describe the path for each so that the team is clear about how choices are made.
- Regain trust and confidence: Demonstrating that there's a clear, structured plan instills confidence in stakeholders, including employees, customers, investors, and the general public. Step-by-step execution will further strengthen confidence levels.

Within these 90 days, set the reporting on the crisis and a cadence for meetings. For example, when you are in the first week of a crisis, you usually do daily reports to measure crisis KPIs. Once the crisis starts to wind down or stabilize (which may even happen within 90 days), shift to 1-2 weeks of weekly reporting. If there are still crisis KPIs to measure beyond this, perhaps report monthly.

Make sure your leadership team, employees, and other stakeholders don't expect the crisis to be over after the 90-day plan. It usually isn't. Executing the plan should help the company be in a better position, but you might need a second plan. This may be for an additional 90 days or perhaps you can move towards a midterm focus with a 120-180-day strategy.

A 90-day plan to raise a late seed-funding round: GoRamp

GoRamp[17] is a Lithuania-headquartered startup providing smart logistics tools. Let's hear from their CEO and co-founder, Jevgenij Polonis, on how they developed a short-term plan to be ready to face different cash constraints scenarios while raising a late seed funding round.

"We had a clear deadline for when adjustments for expenses should be made if we didn't get at least a term sheet from one of the VCs we were negotiating with.

There were two options. Either say nothing until the last minute (when we know the outcome) or communicate it in advance, keeping in mind that for some of the

---

[17] *GoRamp provides a smart logistics tool to optimize your supply chain workflow, warehouse management & dock scheduling. It closed a 3 Mio funding round in July 2023 from several leading VCs in the CEE region and has continued its strong and steady revenue growth.*

teammates, it could bring additional pressure.

We decided to go with the second option. We communicated the deadline. We updated the team on a weekly basis about how many VCs were in the pipeline and the stage they were at. We also made clear what would happen if we weren't able to raise the funds. The most important part of this message was that with only 10-15% cost-cutting, the company would survive even if we weren't successful in raising the round.

We managed to make sure everyone was on the same page. The team even pushed harder because they understood how much their work mattered in the face of the deadlines."

6. Expand your Reach: Leverage multiple channels and formats

One size doesn't fit all when it comes to communication. When dealing with a crisis, work with various communication channels, strategically selected, to generate greater impact. Preferences can be personal, habitual, and generational. While some may be comfortable with email, millennials may love Slack. Generation Z will often prefer videos or maybe connected workplace Notion. When it comes to formats, combine town halls, departmental meetings, and one-on-ones to make sure that everyone understands the message and feels informed and on board. Add further oral and written messages along the way.

Be consistent in your choice of channels so people know where, when, and how they will get information. Where possible, stick to predictable communication patterns that you know work. This will help people feel more at ease.

Increasing the frequency of communication: Startup Wise Guys

Cristobal outlines how Startup Wise Guys changed its communication frequency when times got tough. *"Let me share with you my experience leading Startup Wise Guys in tough times.*

Every Tuesday, we have an operations update where I, together with the leadership team, provide a company update. This includes a CEO update, which is also recorded on Mondays and shared in advance of the call. When times got tough, we gave weekly updates to the entire team. We also agreed that we'd give a financial update every other week.

Normally, you may do this monthly, but in a crisis, you need more frequency.

> In our online monthly strategy all-hands[18], we would share our financials and projections but also explain them in much more detail, opening the floor to questions. A good tip here is to ask managers to collect questions from their teams in advance. Many team members won't feel comfortable asking the CEO questions on a call with the entire company.
>
> It is extremely important to plan and run these meetings under any circumstances. Previous communication should be reviewed to ensure you have addressed any issues and communicated any changes."

Startup Wise Guys runs a range of set meetings and updates that have increased in frequency when different crises have been coming along and hitting the company in different ways (most of them stay after those tough moments):

Type of meeting	Frequency	Format and Channel
Individual Check-Ins	Weekly	Each manager has 15-minute one-to-one Monday calls with direct reports, covering weekly priorities and how they can help.
CEO update	Weekly	Audio recording shared via Slack and WhatsApp

---

[18] "All Hands" refers to meetings where everyone in the company or team is invited. They often encourage active participation in discussions. While these meetings used to be onsite, post-pandemic, many companies run them over Zoom or other online platforms.

Mastering crisis communication

Type of meeting	Frequency	Format and Channel
Operations update	Weekly	Zoom call with the entire team, including a financial update every second week
Operations update summary	Weekly	Minutes of the most important message of the operations update. Email and Slack with links to presentations
Team Check-ins	Weekly	Managers meet with their teams after the operations update, ensuring messages are clear. Questions are collected for the weekly leadership team Zoom call
Strategy Team All Hands	Monthly	Full team half-day meet-up to review performance in the past month and planning and priorities for the next 3 months. Zoom call but with the aim to gather in our offices, with social activities before and after the meeting

7. Learn & Adapt: Use data to understand the effectiveness of crisis communications

"The most important thing in communication is hearing what isn't said"
- *Peter Drucker. Management guru*

Using data to understand and adapt the effectiveness and robustness of communication is an essential strategy for modern organizations. Data-driven insights can help identify areas of strength and weakness in communication and foster continuous improvement. It also diminishes communication bias. In a crisis, data guides the way. It is important to continue measuring effectiveness during a crisis even if it is natural to see a dip in several of the metrics in the initial days and weeks.

Regularly review metrics and adapt communication strategies accordingly. This iterative process ensures that communication strategies remain effective as organizational needs evolve. Crises may force us to both increase the cadence of communications and enable or test new channels. Ensure you can measure the effectiveness of these changes.

Data will also enable you and your team to develop more tailored communication: Different teams or departments may have unique target groups and communication needs. Data can highlight these differences, allowing for more tailored communication strategies.

Some examples of how your use of data can be dialed up in a crisis:

Data Collection Type	Description	Outcome	In a crisis:
Engagement Metrics	Engagement data, such as email open rates, survey response rates, or participation in company events	Attention, reach, and efficiency of communication	Keep a close eye on negative trends or where your workforce may be losing interest. Data points that can help you understand interest levels and perception include: Did the crisis increase employee engagement with the company's content and activities? What content and activities generated higher engagement? Was positive content receiving more or less engagement?

Data Collection Type	Description	Outcome	In a crisis:
Employee Satisfaction and Morale	Regular employee surveys to gauge overall satisfaction and morale. We recommend frequent short surveys that can track sentiments in real time instead of annual surveys. To avoid 'survey fatigue', gamify it, with prizes and leaderboards for the most engaged employees. If you include questions about culture and company, it can also help deepen knowledge about strategic topics and collect relevant data for decision-making. This allows organizations to respond and adapt quickly	Questions about clarity of communication, accessibility of leadership, and understanding of company vision provide specific insights into communication effectiveness.	Surveys can be adapted to help understand The impact of the crisis on morale How employees perceive the crisis itself, the stance of leadership, and the company Whether employees believe in the actions being taken to resolve the issue. See the end of the chapter for details on Motivational mapping as an alternative to this in a crisis and post-crisis

Data Collection Type	Description	Outcome	In a crisis:
Employee Net Promoter Score (ENPS); Enthusiasm and mood surveys (customized versions of ENPS)	ENPS can be applied internally to understand how likely employees are to recommend the company as a workplace to others. This is a measure of loyalty to the company and leadership	A declining internal ENPS might indicate issues with internal communication or company culture.	In a crisis, ENPS is a good tool to help capture the (re)gained trust in the leadership team. Measure shortly after the initial communication. Monitor at 30/60/90 days to test the effect of your internal communication and crisis communication. Questions like "How's your mood today?" or "How's your enthusiasm for the week?" enable you to segment employees into groups (e.g. positive vs. non-positive, or enthusiastic vs. non-enthusiastic) and gain insights by using these segments in new surveys. If the mood of one group is rising while that of another is not, explore the reasons why.

Mastering crisis communication

Data Collection Type	Description	Outcome	In a crisis:
Feedback Platforms	Encourage a culture of feedback using platforms that allow for anonymous submissions.	Employees can voice their concerns or offer suggestions anonymously, removing any potential worries about giving negative feedback.	Increase the frequency of feedback sessions and surveys. Simplify the surveys and adapt them to address crisis-related topics as well. Turn some of the surveys into short, but frequent 1-1 / team meetings to receive feedback firsthand. Make sure you can act on the insight.
Onboarding and Exit Interviews	Feedback from new hires and departing employees is usually performed by the people team and/or hiring managers.	Insight into initial perceptions at onboarding. Exit interviews can highlight long-standing communication challenges	Fundamental in the case of exit interviews. Understand why people leave and any damage from poor communication or understanding

PR and external crisis communication

It is always wise to consult with legal and PR professionals to ensure that communications are appropriate, accurate, and won't lead to unintended consequences. While leaders need to be action-oriented in a crisis, it is worth taking the extra time to pay attention to PR and legal issues.

Having opinions from professionals that you trust will help you understand if the message you are communicating is clear and prepare you for questions. You may need talking points for customer service or account managers, a communication for the board and investors, a communication for employees, a reactive media statement, a statement for social media, and so on. The message needs to be consistent. Make sure everything you are proposing can be executed and provide guidance on realistic timelines.

Using your PR and comms team can also help you understand how your stakeholders and the market are interpreting your moves and how to manage that narrative. And of course, when you reach the unfortunate point of having to consider redundancies, HR and PR will always need to be involved.

External Crisis Communication: How do you prepare?

Zane Bojare is a former Head of Brand at Startup Wise Guys and a communications expert. She also worked for years in a leading PR agency supporting clients with crisis communication. We invited Zane to share learnings from her experience:

Smaller companies that don't have large marketing teams often focus on operations and forget or do not pay enough attention to communication in their crisis planning. Either include communication in your Crisis Management Plan or create a stand-alone Crisis Communication Plan. It doesn't have to be a lengthy document, but put some basics in place to ensure a fast reaction if or when a crisis hits.

The Minimum Viable Crisis Communication Plan: (MVCCP)

Your MVCCP should have these aspects covered:

Who will be communicating on behalf of the company?

- Have at least 2 spokespeople, in case one of them is unavailable when a crisis hits. At least one of them should be a founder or top manager, the second can be from the marketing team
- Spokespeople need regular media training, ideally playing out realistic crisis communication scenarios
- Other team members need to know who the spokespeople are and how they should deal with incoming information requests in a crisis.

Who is on the internal crisis communication team?

- This depends on the company's size, structure, and type of crisis. You would have representatives from top management, marketing, legal, HR, and potentially also IT. You might also want to include a head of the department or business area that is most affected
- To ensure fast agreement and action, don't make this team too big. Depending on company size, limit it to 5-10 people

Who are the key stakeholder groups that need to be informed?

- Have stakeholders' contact details easily accessible
- Employees are often an overlooked key stakeholder group in a crisis. Make internal communication as high a priority as external

- Media should be on your stakeholder list if the crisis has the potential to hit the press. If you work with external PR providers like a freelancer or agency and the crisis has a high risk of causing a PR disaster, consider including a representative in the crisis communication team. Inform them about all the risks and facts as soon as possible.

How do you evaluate the severity of the crisis?
- In the preparatory phase, use the "Risk Impact/Probability Matrix" to assess the risks. On one axis you evaluate the impact and on the other probability.
- Another framework to deploy is the "Crisis Severity Assessment Matrix". You can play with this, but the levels are often ranked from minor to catastrophic and the severity is evaluated based on the potential harm to stakeholders, reputational damage, operational disruption, legal and regulatory implications, and financial impact.

How should you communicate?
- Plan this in line with the Crisis severity assessment. Different levels of crisis should be communicated differently. A minor crisis might just need a memo for employees, a major crisis might need a whole sequence of information flow starting with governmental organizations, journalists, shareholders, etc.
- When you need a strong response, crafting the messages is a form of science. You need to combine. You need to combine empathy, facts, company values, and brand.

Additionally, have on hand some ready-made statements and Questions & Answers documents: Time is of the essence when reacting to a serious crisis and having journalists knocking on your door. You might also want to have some pre-confirmed quotes from the top management if the team is large and it takes longer to confirm communication.

"To speak or not to speak?" That is the question!

One of the biggest challenges in crisis communication is evaluating if the crisis requires a response at all. Sometimes a small incident will lose momentum on its own. By responding you would be shooting yourself in the foot because you might bring more interest than it would attract otherwise

The opposite can also be true, however: not responding fast could be a trigger for escalation. If you are late or not the first one to respond, you are defending and risk not getting your message across. If the audience is already agitated (be it media, clients, or social media followers), you are not communicating in a neutral environment. Your messages are more likely to be misinterpreted.

See for example, the problems Uber had. In 2016 Uber experienced a customer data breach, affecting 57M users. The company did not disclose this information. A year later this incident was covered by the press, severely affecting the company's reputation and bringing legal repercussions.

Mastering crisis communication

"Empathy is at the heart of crisis communication. In moments of adversity, staying human – acknowledging emotions, demonstrating understanding, and showing genuine care – is the key to building trust and resilience."
- Brene Brown

Preparations to neutralize the risk of bad 'break-up' PR: Startup Wise Guys

After concluding work on one investment fund, a four-person team separated from Startup Wise Guys to launch their own regional fund. It was a logical step for the former colleagues, but the local ecosystem and the media seemed to be reading more into the situation. Breakups are often bitter on both sides, even when it is business as usual.

In the spring of 2022, we saw a risk that local ecosystem players might be confused about the relationship between SWG and the former team and the competition between the funds. Together with our PR agency, we drafted a short message "just in case". The original text never saw the light of day: there was no reason to use it.

However, it was instrumental when a few months later a top tech media journalist reached out to our PR representative with rather loaded questions regarding the new fund.

We already had a text template we could adapt and use. Combined with the time that had passed (which allowed us to keep a cool head), it ensured speed in communication. This was useful as journalists don't give you time to develop answers. The final article still contained a whole paragraph on "The Breakup", but it was neutral and it never became an issue.

Key Takeaways

• The tense and stressful environment a crisis creates requires more than our original four pillars of robust communication. In a crisis, ensure you also focus on Transparency & Vulnerability, Reach and Learning & Adapting.

• Be transparent, 100% honest, and open to sharing information. In the face of the stress and skepticism of a crisis, it's fundamental to (re)gain trust.

• Display vulnerability - it can be a powerful communication tool and it makes it easier for employees to relate to you as a leader.

• One size doesn't fit all. Combine multiple channels to expand your reach and ensure that everyone understands the message. Be consistent in your choice of channels so people know where, when, and how they will get information.

• Data-driven insights identify areas of strength and weakness in communication. Ensure you can measure the effectiveness of any communication changes you make.

• Include your PR and comms team to help you understand how the market may interpret your moves and how to manage that narrative.

- Have a Minimum Viable Crisis Communication Plan (MVCCP). Having this basic plan in place ensures a fast reaction if or when the crisis hits and not to be left at the mercy of the situation.

- In a crisis, people will remember how they were treated and how leaders acted more than any specific details. Prioritize open, honest, and empathetic communication to navigate a challenging time, come out stronger, and build trust.

Opportunity Story

Using Motivational Mapping to Reinvigorate a company after a crisis: Startup Wise Guys

One day, the crisis will be over. Hopefully, the company will have survived and be ready to take the next steps on its journey. It will have taken a toll on your team, but there is an opportunity to reinvigorate the company: You can build on the unity and galvanizing energy the team has experienced through the crisis by providing the right motivation for each individual going forward. At Startup Wise Guys we have used Motivational Mapping several times. While it's useful at any time, it can boost recovery post-crisis. Cristobal tells the story of how it all started:

"What motivates you?" is an easy question to answer. However, questions framed in this way often don't elicit meaningful answers, because people have preconceived notions about what the response should be. While useful on an individual level, an open-ended question will also yield a lot of different answers. This can make it very difficult to spot trends within a team or the main motivational factors that are present.

Having gone through one or two crises with our team at Startup Wise Guys, I wanted to avoid the team getting demotivated once the intense, galvanizing period of a crisis was over. We wanted to know how we could re-engage our team and motivate them about the future.

I asked Estonian people and operations expert, Merilin Hehir to help me. Involving the entire leadership team, we started using a new tool: a game of motivational mapping.

It has multiple stacks of cards of intrinsic and extrinsic motivators found in startup and tech teams. These range from 'strong leadership' to 'cool offices' to 'developing expertise'. The moderator leads the "player" through several stacks to uncover their top motivators in a playful way. When these are mapped, they get assessed and analyzed to see how the motivators are met by the company/team/leadership. All members of the team do the exercise. Leaders do it first, so they also learn how to take their teams through it.

I have also added a heatmap to visualize which motivators matter to the team and how often they are mentioned. When leaders better understand their teams' motivations, they can put in place the right company strategies or potential projects to drive the business forward. In addition, it helps employees see their motivators in the company culture and values, and clearly recognise their own motivators in projects that are launched. If their motivators are mapped, leveraged, and revisited through team exercises and sessions from time to time, they will feel significantly more valued."

CHAPTER 4

Letting people go: the hardest part of the CEO's job

In this chapter:

Accepting that you have to let people go

The process: Who has to go and why

Communicating layoffs
- Written communication
- Having a communication gameplan

Offboarding people well

"There is one thing to hate about [a C-suite, founder] role and job: firing people. And it never gets easier. This is most likely the only thing where experience does not help"
- *Jose Leopoldo Alonso, Cristobal´s father*

Letting people go: the hardest part of the CEO's job

"I'll always remember this conversation," says Cristobal. "My father was an executive in several of Spain's largest construction companies and then spent years as an entrepreneur. (Fun fact - he was a classmate of Florentino Perez, Real Madrid's current president.) He was talking about his experience over the years and that sentence remains with me."

Now with over 25 years in management roles and entrepreneurship, Cristobal can only agree. Since the first time he let someone go, in 2004, he has had to do it over and over again. It never gets easier.

At the same time, it is part of your life as a founder and C-level executive. In a crisis, the risk of layoffs is always there - and it all starts in the head of the CEO.

Accepting that you have to let people go

"Layoffs are something you hate to talk about when you first set up your startup. Later it becomes something you must do: it is unfortunately non-negotiable"
- *Liudas Kanapienis, CEO and co-founder, ONDATO*[1]

Layoffs always come as a shock. Sadly, in recent years, redundancies have become more common in the startup and tech scene. After years of hypergrowth,

---

[1] *In our previous book, we introduced Liudas Kanapienis, the CEO and co-founder of Ondato. Ondato is a B2B fintech cybersecurity startup focused on enterprise compliance management. Originally from Lithuania with 2 co-founders and HQ in London. At the end of 2023, the company had 130 employees and nearly 600k monthly revenues and it is seen by many as one of the future Lithuanian unicorns to come.*

the contrast is painful.

A crisis in a startup often arises due to financial hardship - and startup finances are particularly sensitive to any overall societal or market issues. Therefore, redundancies are often part and parcel of a crisis.

As you will have gathered, we are strong believers in culture and people as fundamental to the success of a startup. With this attitude, CEOs try to find solutions to reduce costs or increase the cash position rather than "just" letting people go. This can include offering furloughs or shortened workweeks and hours, eliminating waste, doing away with non-essential (pet) projects, or redeploying workers to other units based on transferable skills. Often, co-founders and C-suite cut their salaries dramatically in order to avoid layoffs, but sometimes redundancies are unavoidable.

This is not letting people go because of team members' individual performance, but because of the company's performance. In fact, in many cases letting people go means the CEO is accepting failure, or that they've made a wrong decision. There comes a point when you have to accept that not making redundancies is going to put you and the rest of the company and team at peril. Letting some people go is the price to pay for being able to keep others and have a chance to stay afloat with those who remain.

Mentally handling this crisis is a very painful part of the job which is often not talked about. Especially if it is your first CEO crisis, existential questions are inevitable. Is this my fault? What have I done wrong? Why have I allowed it to get to this point? Am I good enough to be the CEO? Does it even make sense to continue fighting and going through this kind of pain and stress? All these questions will be there. And yes, you have invested all your time, energy, and effort to bring the business to the place where it is today, but this is where you are now. It is CEO and leadership time.

It may seem like it is your fault that the business is in a crisis. You have undoubtedly played a part, but the odds are that the reason isn't you alone. Countless people in the team, internal and external factors add up. Don't be too hard on yourself - everyone makes mistakes. No one can predict the market. The main question is "What has to be done to have a working business 3 or 6 months from now, so you are still in a position to make new mistakes in the future (= the shop is still running)"?

You need to accept the current situation and understand what will happen if you have a positive answer to that question. It is essential that the company continues operating, of course, but it will also become much leaner and more agile. There could be new energy. Those who remain will build a stronger team and product going forward.

Accepting the inevitable: Alexandru Stan, CEO at Tekpon

"Unfortunately, I have been in a situation where I have to let people go - even the entire company. That may sound terrifying, but being a CEO is not about having the top position in the company and the best office while others work for you and your needs. It's a demanding job, like being a king in a kingdom and caring for every person living there. If they are not living well, it is your fault. It is about people.

Having to let people go is hard. This isn't just about informing them, but about the ripple effects that the decision creates in their lives and the company. It's a weight that sits heavily on me. I carry it with a deep sense of responsibility and empathy.

In 2017, a crisis shook my company to its core. We were growing at an unprecedented rate and hiring quickly, all due to the increased demand for our products. However, the situation wasn't as perfect as it seemed. The rapid expansion brought significant financial strain, making it difficult for us to keep up with payroll payments. Despite our best efforts, the business was no longer sustainable. We could see bankruptcy looming over us like a dark cloud.

As a leader, the weight of my decisions was always heavy. I remember countless nights of tossing and turning, the stress gnawing at my conscience. These were not just employees but unique individuals with families, passions, and aspirations.

When the moment arrived, I knew I had to handle it with utmost care and compassion. I gathered my courage and devised a plan to mitigate the impact as much as possible. For the top performers and those with specialized skills, I contacted my network to help them find jobs in other companies. There was some comfort in knowing that I could assist some people in transitioning to new opportunities.

For others, the journey took a different turn. I made

the bold decision to start a new company and offered those willing the opportunity to embark on this new venture with me. It was a leap of faith, for them and me, but it was an opportunity to rebuild and create something new from our past efforts.

Letting people go is not just a business decision; it's deeply personal and has profound effects on lives. As a CEO, it's crucial to handle such situations with empathy and support. The hardest part of being a CEO is not the strategic decisions or the financial pressures; it's the human element. It's about caring for your team, making tough decisions with compassion, and leading with both your head and your heart. In the end, it's this balance that defines true leadership"

The process - who has to go and why

Letting people go: the hardest part of the CEO's job

"I have a rule for myself which I am also repeating all the time to my co-founders and management team. If you wake up in the morning and think that 'without that person in the team, you would be ok', you just have to let that person go straight away. Every person you work with needs to be needed"
- Liudas Kanapienis, CEO and co-founder, Ondato

It is hard to let go of things, projects, and people. Emotions more often than not play a part in these situations. In a crisis, it is important to:

• Zoom out and think logically: What are the goals in the short term, to give the company a fighting chance in the long term? Don't forget your company values and try not to cut corners with this company options´ assessment process;

• Think about people and projects from the perspective of value add. Who can make the biggest impact in this fight for survival? What projects can be put on hold, as they won't get you closer to the mission-critical goals in the near future?

Once you have identified that you need to downsize, how do you go about it? Use this simple, clear roadmap:

1. Set clear objectives

Define the goals and objectives of the restructuring or downsizing. Be specific about the company aims you are looking to achieve as a consequence

2. Analyze current staffing

Evaluate the current workforce, considering factors like skills, performance, roles, and responsibilities. Determine which positions are essential for the company's short-term goals to generate cash so that it has a shot at survival. Try to re-hire / re-purpose some of the laid-off people in the long term if possible. Also, take a look at your core product needs and evaluate them. You need to make sure you don't cut staff needed to continue the development of your cash-generating product or service, nor the support for the version your customers are currently using. Focus instead on cutting all the experimental, non-performing, or unclear parts and functionalities.

3. Establish criteria

Develop criteria for selecting employees who will be affected by the changes. Criteria can include factors like job performance, skills, seniority, and cost-effectiveness. There is often an option to cut middle management layers, to save as much working power as possible and flatten the structure. This can be a significant savings opportunity and can improve the relationship between the leaders and the team. Being closer to the team enables leaders to react quickly if the mood in the company changes. It creates more work for top management, but that is the price to pay when times get tough.

4. Assess and Rank Employees

Apply the established criteria to evaluate employees.

Create a ranked list of employees based on these criteria.

5. Decision-Making

Use the ranked list to make informed decisions about who will be affected by the changes. Ensure that decisions are fair and consistent with the established criteria.

Throughout this process, ensure legal compliance: All decisions must adhere to labor laws, regulations, and contractual obligations. Consult with legal counsel to avoid legal pitfalls.

Communicating layoffs

Layoffs are never easy - neither for those having to deliver the message nor those receiving it. The key to making it as tolerable as possible is, yet again, communication and a bulletproof plan. Keep in mind that you may need to adapt your communication style, whether written or verbal, depending on the cultural background of the team and the person, the national traits of your people, or the company business culture and/or the country of operations. This can make a huge difference, in the way the message is perceived and digested

You met Tom Niparts, CEO & Co-founder of JeffApp in a previous chapter. He emphasized some key aspects of how to communicate when making redundancies. Many of his comments echo our points in the previous chapter:

"When facing even the prospect of layoffs, three

things to me are non-negotiable on the communications front:

- Total transparency is the policy. The best thing to do is to apply it from Day One. The second best thing is to apply it from Today. Without key information - details of where the financial issues sit - the team can't focus on what matters. If you don't feel safe disclosing the true picture, you need to change your team.
- Manage expectations. If you have money for five months, be honest that stretching it to 8 months will mean layoffs in 4-8 weeks if the ship is not turning around. Don't be afraid if someone leaves with this info at hand: They have less skin in the game than you may have initially thought. And vice versa - tough times create strong teams and uncover some overlooked talent.
- Give relevant context and ensure you have more than a Plan A to get back on track. Not explaining how you ended up here and how you will get out is a sure recipe for a drop in confidence and spike in chaos."

Written communication

In May 2020, Brian Chesky, co-founder and CEO of Airbnb, communicated a large round of layoffs due to the impact of COVID-19[2]. The note is personal, transparent, and explanatory and brings Airbnb values to the table. It begins:

"This is my seventh time talking to you from my house. Each time we've talked, I've shared good news

---

[2] Thum, Y. (2022, March 3). *5 key learnings from Airbnb's layoff Note by CEO, Brian Chesky*. Medium. https://medium.com/@yeelinthum/5-things-companies-can-learn-from-airbnbs-layoff-letter-by-ceo-brian-chesky-1664068c2a87

Letting people go: the hardest part of the CEO's job

and bad news, but today I have to share some very sad news.

When you've asked me about layoffs, I've said that nothing is off the table. Today, I must confirm that we are reducing the size of the Airbnb workforce. For a company like us whose mission is centered around belonging, this is incredibly difficult to confront, and it will be even harder for those who have to leave Airbnb. I am going to share as many details as I can on how I arrived at this decision, what we are doing for those leaving, and what will happen next".

The summarized breakdown of Brian Chesky's message to the Airbnb employees provides a great example of written communication to a company facing layoffs:

Introduction
- Acknowledgment of layoff
- Company Mission
- List of what will be covered in the note

The situation
- What's happening?
- How is this affecting the company?
- What was the conclusion?
- Why was the decision made?
- What was the decision-making process?
  For the laid-off employees
- Details of severance, equity, healthcare, and job support

What will happen next
- Details of how employees will know if they stay or are getting laid off
- CEO Q&A session
- Conclusion
- Words of gratitude
- Reiteration of the company mission
- Note for those staying
- Note for those leaving

Having a communications gameplan

Our good friend, Estonian people and operations expert Merilin Hehir[3], has already been introduced in the previous chapter. She was Head of People and Operations at a company that experienced hypergrowth (close to 10x within a year) but later had to make at least 10% of the staff redundant. Making redundancies is always painful, but she aimed to make sure that people felt respected and taken care of at a difficult time, while her operational process complied with all requirements.

Every layoff is unique and requires specific considerations but this game plan from Merilin can work in a small or medium-sized company.

Steps to take and what to consider:

1. Get your operations/HR/legal team involved as soon as possible. They will do the majority of the one-to-one

---

[3] Merilin Hehir, People and Business Operations, Lucky Otter https://www.linkedin.com/in/merilinhehir/

communication, support people through the layoff procedure, and alleviate any worries.

2. Keep managers whose teams will be affected in the loop. Don't make their decisions for them unless you have to. The leader may have ideas about who to let go, but team leads know best. However, decide on the key criteria that should be considered when deciding who to make redundant.

3. The people affected should always be told the news first. Decide when to do this, and when to inform the rest of the company. This should happen as soon as possible afterward, at an in-person meeting or company-wide call. I have used a timestamped plan:

Example
- 10:00 Notification for a company-wide meeting later during the day (just say that it's an important announcement and you expect everyone to attend).
- 10:00 - 14.00 Start breaking the news to people laid off.
- 14:00 Company-wide meeting where you break the news to everyone.

Make sure you:
- Schedule an in-person meeting/call. If at all possible, do not let people know they face redundancy via email.
- Never schedule the meeting with those affected in advance (e.g. sending the message on a Friday to have the meeting on a Monday). Do it on the day, to prevent

Letting people go: the hardest part of the CEO's job

speculation and panic. People may guess the topic regardless of what you call the meeting
- Include the Founder/CEO/Top leadership and direct manager in the call to those affected. If you have several people in the top leadership who can break the news, divide them to save time and avoid news spreading and taking on a life of its own.

Get a script and a checklist ready to tell those affected about the redundancy. It's a stressful situation with unexpected reactions. Having a script will ensure that no crucial detail is missed. Talk it through with your operations/HR/legal team.
- Break the news first, then explain. There's no need to keep people waiting in anticipation of the only thing they will remember from this very painful call.
- Be straightforward, honest, empathic, and supportive. Leave space for their questions. Offer your support in giving recommendations for a new job.
- Let them know the HR/legal team is there to offer further explanation.

4. Check up on the people laid off after a few days. This offers comfort and shows respect. Ongoingly check up on the people who weren't laid off as well.

People who remain on the team will have questions. Be open to answering these both in the meeting and privately. This is the time to show empathy, direction, and reassurance.

As a CEO, with your leadership team, you need to be

prepared to tackle some key questions, both for your own planning and queries from the team.

To plan for:
- How do we (re) establish trust?
- How do we rally them around the short-term objectives? (see also motivational mapping example in Robust Communication chapter)
- How do we motivate the team in the current crisis landscape?

To respond to your team:
- Why should they stay with more work, more stress, and likely less pay?
- Why are they the ones chosen to stay?

While the detailed answers from each leader may sound different, there should only be one core message. Refer back to the principles we've outlined in the Robust Communication chapter - you can use them repeatedly in your communication.

Letting people go: the hardest part of the CEO's job

Offboarding departing employees

Chesky's note for AirBnB employees also showed care and demonstrates how to show who you truly are when you let people go:

"To take care of those that are leaving, we have looked across severance, equity, healthcare, and job support and done our best to treat everyone in a compassionate and thoughtful way".

Some hold the view that you should be firm rather than good to staff that are leaving. In the startup world, there is a high chance that team members will either go on to start their own business, cross paths with you in the future, or continue to have a positive impact in the startup ecosystem. This is why it is not only morally right but also makes sense for you personally to help them transition away from your business.

If you have to let go of staff because of downsizing, it is often no fault of their own. They will likely be loyal, hard-working, and give huge value to another company.

Letting people go: the hardest part of the CEO's job

Practically this means giving them a fair notice period, with an outline of your offboarding process and your commitment to them. As noted in the case study below: promote their skills on social media and leverage your network to make introductions.

Finally, maintain the relationship. Reach out to them to see if you can help them or give them advice. Remember the stress that they went through to help you to build your company. They deserve every bit of support you can give them to move on.

Offboarding people well: Patrick Collins

Patrick Collins[4], sales coach and CEO and a long-term Startup Wise Guys collaborator, notes the importance of offboarding people well:

"When companies say they are a 'family' then they should treat people like this when they leave. This means it is the responsibility of the company to ensure the staff member has all the resources and support they need to move on to the next chapter of their life," notes Patrick.

He personally invests time ensuring departing team members' CVs are updated - highlighting the projects where they have excelled. He ensures that there are testimonials on their CV/ LinkedIn so they can show social proof. You may also give genuine feedback and advice on their skills and what you think the next career move can be.

---

[4] *Patrick Collins is a founder, growth advisor, and entrepreneur with over 10 years of experience in helping startups scale and succeed. He is the founder of Prospect-Labs, a B2B lead generation software that went from 0 to 27K in monthly revenue in the first 13 months.*

Letting people go: the hardest part of the CEO's job

"Make a LinkedIn post talking about why this person is so important to you, the great work they did, and how they would be so good at any new company they join. Let people know they are available to join a new company and to enquire if they would like to speak to them. With this and referrals you can often have a member of staff have a new job within the week you give them notice", says Patrick.

Like in sales, referrals are the most powerful way to make an introduction to let other companies know that you have staff available. Think of this as not job hiring but a job 'firing' board where people can see who is available from your company. While it may seem like a wacky idea, it has worked for Patrick in the past. Your staff might already have a direct relationship with them and so the possibility of hiring them full-time could appeal. Patrick relates a story of a successful referral:

"Gintare[5] worked for me at Prospect Labs for just under a year, in customer support. When my business changed and I realized that I needed to scale down my company, I was unfortunately in a position where I had to give her notice. Dux-Soup (a large LinkedIn automation software tool) was one of our main clients. Gin had been working with them directly. I asked the founder if he would be interested in hiring her and he accepted instantly. I said that with the skills she had there would be a lot of companies wanting to hire her. He hired her instantly with a higher wage than what I was paying her.

---

[5] *Gintare Kuzminskaitė, Head of Customer Support, Dux-Soup,* https://www.linkedin.com/in/gin-kuz/

Letting people go: the hardest part of the CEO's job

Gin has been at Dux-Soup now for over 4 years and is head of customer support. Every couple of months I catch up with her and she updates me on new LinkedIn rules and changes and ensures that I am fully prepared to apply to my sales training. Keeping a good relationship with Gin has ensured that her career continued to develop and given me an expert source of information to stay up to date with LinkedIn, which is directly relevant to my business. Win-win for everyone."

As CEO and leader, take good care of the people leaving when forced to make redundancies - there's opportunity in well-executed redundancies. Your company will be leaner, more agile, and have new energy, so those who remain can build a stronger company, team, and product.

"...Tough times create strong teams and uncover some overlooked talent"

- Tom Niparts, CEO and co-founder, JeffApp

Key Takeaways

• In a crisis, the need to let people go is usually the outcome of many internal and external factors. As CEO, you must learn how to accept when you have reached this point.

• Layoffs are never easy. Consider who should be laid off. Evaluate factors like value-add, essential roles, and immediate business needs in the decision-making process.

• The keys to making it as tolerable as possible for everyone involved are communication and a bulletproof plan. Place emphasis on honesty, transparency, and proactive communication in delivering layoff news and managing employee expectations

• Think of the people who remain. Do not forget they will most likely have questions and need reassurance so be open to answering these both in meetings and privately. This is the time to show empathy, direction, and reassurance.

• Support during transition is vital. It is important to provide resources, support, and networking opportunities for departing employees to facilitate their career transition.

• Maintain positive relationships with departing employees and support them beyond their tenure with the company by leveraging your network and making introductions to other companies, letting them know you have staff available.

• While extremely difficult, layoffs may be an opportunity to re-energize and create a leaner, more flexible, and focused workforce

Opportunity Story

The future is bright after pivoting and downsizing, Sellfy

Maris Dagis is the CEO of Sellfy, a Latvia headquartered company helping digital content creators maximize monetization. In its early days, the company faced a major crisis after pivoting its business model in the search for hypergrowth. Maris tells the story:

"Our biggest crisis was in 2015 when we made an unsuccessful pivot from an e-commerce platform for digital goods to a marketplace. When we made the decision, our hypothesis was that it would allow us to grow at a much higher rate. We also raised additional capital for this move.

After spending a year developing and kick-starting the marketplace, initial traction was not good. We found ourselves in a situation where we were running out of funds. Because of the unsuccessful pivot, there was very little chance for us to raise more money. We needed to extend our runway to make another pivot to profitability. We:

Identified key personnel crucial for executing a successful pivot and ensuring the company's survival.

Held an all-hands meeting to openly address our strategic missteps, presented data on our business performance, and proposed a new plan to get to profitability.

Acknowledged the necessity of further pivot and

unfortunately, communicated the need for layoffs.

Leveraged open communication and transparency to foster understanding among team members, mitigating the negative impact of layoffs.

In the end, we had a smaller but very motivated team that successfully made another pivot to a sustainable business model that continues to work successfully even today."

CHAPTER 5

Managing your mental state & leading your team

In this chapter:

Support structures: Equipping yourself to deal with difficulties

Three areas for a leader to keep strong at all times
- Body
- Mind
- Support Network

Staying in control in stressful times
- Finding your own reboot tools

Leading your team in times of crisis

"There are no stressful situations. Only stressful responses."
- Howard Behar, former president of Starbucks International

Managing your mental state & leading your team

As an entrepreneur, you are navigating uncertainty on a daily basis. It is part of your job. In many ways, you are much better equipped to deal with emergencies and crises than others, because you have to do it on an ongoing basis.

Your mental state can have a big effect on your decision-making. A crisis is stressful. Understanding how your body and mind react to stress can be an important part of your effort to control it.

Our stress response system reacts to perceived threats. When it detects a threat, it switches to survival mode. It speeds up our heartbeat to increase blood flow, and our breathing to take in more oxygen. It slows digestion to store fat and sugar for energy. When our senses detect danger, the amygdala is activated. It is the emotional center of the brain. When it perceives a threat, it sends stress signals to another part of your brain, the prefrontal cortex, to limit its activities.

All of this can be very helpful in situations that require an urgent response, but it can play havoc with our capability to think straight, instead making us act on impulse. This is because the prefrontal cortex is the so-called control center of our brains. It helps us to control our thoughts, actions, and emotional responses. It's in charge of the rational reasoning that kicks in when we take a moment and wait instead of acting on instinct, fuelled by that quickening pulse.

The most effective founders learn to stay in control and make rational decisions even in the most stressful conditions. To do this, you need to find a way to move past your stress response and into a place where your prefrontal cortex can re-engage.

Legendary martial arts actor and philosopher Bruce Lee[1] used a metaphor that captures this well: "Empty your mind, be formless. Shapeless, like water. If you put water into a cup, it becomes the cup. You put water into a bottle and it becomes the bottle. You put it in a teapot, it becomes the teapot. Now, water can flow or it can crash. Be water, my friend."

Instead of trying to fight the circumstances and events we cannot control, Lee recommends we adapt and not let them affect us - at least not for long. Like water, we can become one with the situation and adapt to it.

In 2017 Stoyan attended a 10-day silent meditation retreat - Vipassana. Not being allowed to speak, write, or have interactions with anyone allows your sensibili-

---

[1] Source: McBride, T.L. (2013, 15 August). Bruce Lee Be As Water My Friend. YouTube. https://youtu.be/cJMwBwFj5nQ?si=xMWu9luFOo6iwztm

ty to heighten. Being confined in this way and meditating for 10-11 hours each day gave Stoyan space to observe himself, his mind, his thoughts, and his emotions. One of his key realizations was how much our mind is running on autopilot on a daily basis and how easily we can get triggered. Importantly, he also realized how much you can strengthen your mind and your ability to manage yourself. Like building muscle in the gym, your ability to manage your mind and your mental state can also be trained.

In this chapter, we will explore what you can do as a founder to manage your mental state and lead your team effectively in a crisis.

Support structures: Equipping yourself to deal with difficulties

An effective leader should be prepared for something going wrong at any moment. The founder of Reebok, Joe Foster noted to us[2]: "...Whilst you are not looking to fail, just be prepared. Things will happen. You could fail. You're certainly going to have a lot of problems on the road. If you don't have problems, then goodness...I don't know where and how you manage to do that."

It took Foster and his brother 21 years to scale Reebok to a global player. They successfully entered the American market after at least 6 failed attempts, multiple challenges, and difficulties. In the end, it was all

---

[2] Source: Yankov, S. (2021, June 10). *Reebok: The Untold Story of Building an Iconic Global Brand with Joe Foster. Productivity Mastery.* YouTube. https://www.youtube.com/watch?v=CFNNfWthGIw

worth it - Reebok became the #1 sports brand in the world in the 80s.

It's easier to endure difficulties when you have the right support structures in place. We are always looking for the easy fix or the one secret strategy that will solve all our problems, but it's usually the fundamentals that make the difference.

Three areas for a leader to keep strong at all times

1. Body

Elon Musk may not be in optimal physical shape, but he's an exception to the rule. Most highly productive founders understand it's almost necessary to be in great shape.

Physical fitness is positively correlated to stress resilence[3]. Here is something fascinating: Finnish researchers[4] found that people who exercise regularly tend to make more money. The study followed 5,000 male twins for almost thirty years. By tracking who was active and who was sedentary, they determined that regular exercise contributed to 14-17% higher long-term income levels. According to the researchers, exercise: "make[s] people more persistent in the face of work-related difficulties, and increase their desire to engage in competitive situations."

**Daily Workout Routine to endure difficulties:
Marian Temelkov, Dynamis Group[5]**

"I never skip a workout. In 2019 the team and I went through our most challenging year. We went through a buyout and had extremely ambitious financial objectives to reach in order to survive as a company. Problems were coming from everywhere. It was a constant fight for survival for a good 12 months. What helped me stay sane was my exercise routine. No matter how hectic my days were, I would hit the gym every morning at 7:00 am and do my workout. And only once I'd completed it, I would turn into "working mode" and address all

---

[3] *Source: Neumann, R. J., Ahrens, K. F., Kollmann, B., Goldbach, N., Chmitorz, A., Weichert, D., Fiebach, C. J., Wessa, M., Kalisch, R., Lieb, K., Tüscher, O., Plichta, M. M., Reif, A., & Matura, S. (2021). The impact of physical fitness on resilience to modern life stress and the mediating role of general self-efficacy. European Archives of Psychiatry and Clinical Neuroscience, 272(4), 679–692.* https://doi.org/10.1007/s00406-021-01338-9

[4] *Source: Hyatt, M. (2015, March 23). Why exercising now matters for your future. Full Focus.* https://fullfocus.co/exercising-matters-for-your-future/

[5] *Dynamis Group, a global executive search firm founded in Manchester, the UK in 2019, unites leaders through strategic network development and forming extraordinary teams.*

the challenges. When difficult times hit, people tend to cut down on self-care, exercise, and proper nutrition. It's exactly when you should double down on it. Build the habit today and be even more disciplined with it in a crisis. It's not just good for you. It's your responsibility to your team and startup. And don't come out with the excuse that you don't have the time. You make the time because it matters."

It can be difficult for a busy founder to sustain a solid workout regime and a healthy diet.

The key is to keep things simple. Make it easy to follow through. Here are a few ideas you can borrow:

- Join a gym or fitness center near your home or office. It's easier to incorporate exercise into your daily routine if you don't have to go out of your way.
- Hire a personal trainer or get a fitness buddy. Having someone to hold you accountable makes you more likely to stick to your workout schedule.
- Join group fitness classes. Whether it's CrossFit, HIIT, or Yoga, structured group classes provide motivation and support from fellow participants, making it easier to stay committed.
- Choose a sport that is fun. For Stoyan this is squash. Cristobal plays basketball. As the element of fun increases so does your motivation to exercise regularly.
- Only buy healthy snacks. By keeping only healthy snacks readily available, you reduce the temptation to indulge in less nutritious options, as you'd have to make an effort to obtain them.

2. Mind

We are hardwired to focus on the negative[6], as outlined in Chapter 1. We remember traumatic experiences better than positive ones and respond more strongly to negative events. This was a great strategy for primitive prehistoric humans, as it helped them avoid danger. It's not always helpful in modern times. Entrepreneurship is filled with hiccups and setbacks. Strengthen your mind daily by intentionally guiding it to stay objective and not go into negativity spirals. Train your mind to stay focused on the positive and to look for solutions and opportunities.

Do this by reading inspiring articles, business- and leadership books (or watching videos and TV shows like Shark Tank[7], if that's your cup of tea!). Listen to insightful podcasts and audiobooks. Build a meditation or mindfulness practice. Learn from those who are ahead of you in the areas where you want to improve. One of the main reasons Stoyan hosts his own podcast[8] is that he gets to spend an hour every week learning from some of the most successful people in their areas. Find your equivalent practice.

---

[6] *Source: MSEd, K. C. (2023b, November 13). What is the negativity bias?. Verywell Mind.* https://www.verywellmind.com/negative-bias-4589618#citation-2

[7] *Shark Tank is a television format in which entrepreneurs present their business ideas to a panel of investors, known as the Sharks. These investors include prominent figures that assess the pitches and choose if they want to invest their own capital if they find the opportunities promising. Source:* https://www.cnbc.com/shark-tank/

[8] *Productivity Mastery is a podcast hosted by Stoyan Yankov, where unicorn founders, entrepreneurs, top-level executives and best selling authors share their habits, strategies and mindsets.* https://stoyanyankov.com/podcast/

Cut out all distractions and negativity: GERMAN COPPOLA, YUMIWI[9]

"Your phone is your biggest distraction. You open it and immediately get bombarded with useless notifications, negativity, and junk. A few years ago I decided to switch off all notifications on my phone. Now I have to specifically open an app to see news and updates. When I open my phone the first three screens are filled with applications that are there to nurture my mind: meditation apps, audiobooks, journaling tools, and everything else that will support me and my growth.

I usually wake up early. I do not check any emails, news, or updates for the first two hours. This is my time to read, learn, and grow. Then I have breakfast with my family, I fill myself with positivity and I am ready to take on the challenges the day presents me. Once you build the habit, it gets easier to follow through and you never want to go back."

3. Support network

Build a network of people who have your back. This begins with strengthening your relationship with your cofounders. That should be your safety net. But also look at helping and supporting other entrepreneurs and business leaders. Nurture strong relationships with like-minded people. It is time well spent because when difficult times occur you will have people to rely on.

---

[9] *YUMIWI is an event management software developer, based in Madrid, Spain in 2014. Their belief is that the attendees' experience is everything, that's why they offer tools to engage with them at all stages of events.*

Many successful founders create "mastermind groups" or private circles with other like-minded leaders. In these groups, they can freely share their struggles and feelings, and receive support and practical advice. Who are the people you can rely on in a crisis? Maybe you want to consider setting up an advisory board, joining a business club, or hiring a coach. Build strong support structures so that when a crisis hits, you have someone there to give you help and advice.

Surround yourself with a supportive peer group: Viktoriya Vasilenko, Knowledge Gate Group[10]

"When I go through stressful times, it's the people around me that lift me up. Early on in my entrepreneurial journey, I realized how difficult it is to be a founder. So I took the time and energy to build a strong group of other entrepreneurs. We meet up regularly and talk about our struggles and challenges. It's a safe, non-judgmental place because we are all on a similar journey. Now, every time I go through difficulties I have people I can call who understand me and want to help me. They have been there for me many times and helped me go through my hardest moments."

---

[10] Knowledge Gate Group is an AI platform developer that helps identify and connect organizations to scientific opinion leaders. It was founded in Copenhagen, Denmark in 2020

Staying in control in stressful times

Dealing with sudden disaster: Starbucks

It's 3:00 am. Howard Behar is sleeping in his apartment in the Seattle area. As the president of Starbucks, he had a long day at work. Suddenly the telephone rings. It's the regional vice president, calling him from Washington DC. He doesn't waste time. *"We had a disaster,"* he says. Behar knows something terrible has happened. It turns out someone entered one of the Starbucks stores and killed the 3 employees working there. How do you show up when a disaster like that happens? You are not always going to be prepared. Sometimes bad news and crises will hit you when you are least prepared, overwhelmed, and exhausted. But it's your actions in a crisis that will determine who you are as a leader. Great leaders face the situation head-on. They find their inner mental strength, pull themselves together, and do their best to lead the team towards a solution.

Howard Behar immediately calls his CEO Howard Schulz, who is on the East Coast. Schulz decides to share everything he knows with the media, providing clarity and taking ownership. In the next few days, he personally visits all three families of the young people killed. Starbucks makes sure the colleagues of the victims are taken care of, hiring counselors and paying each employee while they can't work. Starbucks closed the affected store for a while. Once it was opened again, they donated all profits to non-violence in Washington DC. *"In that kind of a crisis, you have to be an authentic,*

> *vulnerable human being and understand that people are in pain. And deal with that, in an honest way,"* says Behar.

When a crisis hits it can be difficult to find your composure. In fact, humans often act strangely in such circumstances. In BBC footage of the 2011 Japanese earthquake[11], people risked their lives to save bottles of alcohol from breaking in a supermarket. When an airplane caught fire at an airport in Denver in 2023, the evacuation of passengers slowed down due to people watching the flames and taking selfies. John Leach is a psychologist at the University of Portsmouth who survived the fire at London's Kings Cross in 1987[12]. He estimates that in a crisis, 80-90% of people respond inappropriately[13], for example by freezing when evacuation is necessary. He advocates for survival training to overcome the cognitive constraints such extreme situations bring with it - just like practicing your mental toughness ahead of time will help in a crisis.

It seems to be against our nature to act normally in a crisis. That should be an even bigger motivation for you to learn to take control when challenging times hit your

---

[11] *"On March 11, 2011, Japan experienced the strongest earthquake in its recorded history. Source: Tohoku earthquake and tsunami. (n.d.).* https://education.nationalgeographic.org/resource/tohoku-earthquake-and-tsunami/

[12] *"The King's Cross Fire in November 1987 was the worst fatal fire that has ever been seen on the London Underground." Source:* www.btp.police.uk/police-forces/british-transport-police/areas/about-us/about-us/our-history/the-kings-cross-fire-of-1987/

[13] Source: *Why people "freeze" in an emergency: temporal and cognitive constraints on survival responses. (2004, June 1). PubMed.* https://pubmed.ncbi.nlm.nih.gov/15198281/

startup. Panic and stress will try to take over. Don't let that happen. Find your calm.

Some of you might remember a time when computers weren't that fast. If you were using them for a while, they would heat up. You had no choice but to hit the reboot button. Once restarted, the computer would operate normally again. Sometimes, the computer was so overheated that you needed to shut it down and wait a few minutes before turning it on again.

What helps YOU to reboot, personally?

For some of you it can be:
- Closing your eyes and doing breathing exercises for a few minutes
- Taking a break and going for a short walk to clear your thoughts
- Going for a run
- Sharing the challenge with someone from your support network, seeking advice and perspective on the issue
- Opening your notebook and journaling your thoughts
- Listening to a specific song that brings you back to a better mental state

Doing the best you can today: Ilma Tiki, MailerLite

"I think the most important thing during a crisis is to first breathe in, to breathe out, and not to freak out, because the things you do during a crisis are the things that will have an impact in the long term. So it's really important to stick to your own values, instead of just freaking out and pretending that everything is fine. So I think it's really important to calm yourself down and understand that it's part of business, it's part of life. And remember where you are coming from, what you believe in, and what you can do right now. What is the best you can do today?"

- Ilma Tiki, co-founder of MailerLite

Tony Robbins, a world-renowned performance coach and leadership advisor, says the fastest way to change your mental state is by changing your physiology. During one of his seminars, Joseph McLendon III, who works closely with Robbins, asked the audience to do a simple exercise. Try it yourself:

1. Stand up
2. Put on a big smile
3. Stand in a superhero posture
4. (Very important) Start moving your ass to the left and right in a cheerful manner.
Once you have achieved all 4 previous steps it's time for the final one:
5. Try to feel depressed! Exactly. You can't.

It's impossible to be in a state of joy and laughter and feel bad at the same time. We're not suggesting you do this exact exercise every time things get tough. Find your own tools. Whatever works, use it. Your team will rely on you to show up and lead them with a cool head.

Sometimes we freeze. We fail to decide because we are afraid we might make a mistake. But failing to decide is a decision in itself. And in crises and emergencies, it can be fatal.

Marilyn Zakhour found a mental trick to deal with that fear.

82% Grace: Marilyn Zakhour, Cosmic Centaurs

Since becoming a mom, Marilyn, the founder and CEO of Cosmic Centaurs has started a new mantra: 82% grace. While in the past she would aim for perfection (or more) she now accepts what is arguably a high error rate of 18% and gives herself grace when her actions fall in that 18%. This applies to all aspects of her life: work, parenting, friendships. Adjusting to 82% grace (instead of 100%) allows her to maintain a level of excellence where it matters while spending the time she saves with her daughter.

Leading your team in times of crisis

What happens when your startup is finally doing well and suddenly your country is in a state of war?

Leading your team and growing your startup in times of war: Finmap

Ivan Kaunov is a co-founder of Finmap[14], a cash flow management tool that allows business owners to be clear over their company's financial state without special knowledge of finance. At the beginning of 2021, things were looking good for the startup. Ivan and his team of 60 finally closed a €1,2 million round, making them ready to scale advertising and sales. Then, in an instant, everything changed. Ivan tells the story:

"I remember vividly the morning of February 24, 2022. I was woken up in my apartment in Kyiv by the noise of explosions. Sirens came only a couple of hours later. No one was expecting what happened.

I looked outside. I couldn't believe what I saw. I checked my phone and my social media accounts were

---

[14] Finmap is based in Kiev, Ukraine and was founded in 2017. It is now reaching more than 50 countries with more than 15 million transactions being processed so far.

filled with news about the Russian Federation's invasion of Ukraine, my country.

I didn't even have time to pack our bags. First I had to calm my wife down. I took a minute to create an action plan and explain it to her so that she felt that I knew what to do and was in control.

I told her she had to pack one bag, water the flowers, and pack our dog's stuff. Even if we didn't need everything from that list, it gave me at least 15 minutes and minimized her stress, since she was taking actions that were in her control. We left our apartment in Kyiv immediately and drove to my dad's house outside the city. During the drive, I explained the next steps - with calm and ease, as if nothing was happening. The trick is to be calm and show that you know what to do.

You can't prepare for an event like this. Even though it was a possibility, and we had an emergency plan prepared, you can never fully comprehend what is happening.

I called my co-founder Alex. Finmap had been working as a fully remote company for a long time, so we had a lot of employees throughout the country: Bucha, Irpin, Kharkiv, Kherson, Berdyansk, and Zaporizhzhia. We had to take care of them. I hadn't slept much and had a bit of a headache, but there was no time to think of myself. When a crisis happens you need to get yourself together and address the problems immediately.

We recognised that the biggest priority was to help people evacuate from the most dangerous regions. We quickly made a list of what needed to be done and started executing it. The priorities were to communicate the *news and updates to everyone and reach out individually to help evacuate our people. It was a mess because nobody knew what was happening. Imagine your entire country being attacked. Where do you even evacuate to? But you have to stay strong and provide your team with direction and certainty. Alex and I looked for every opportunity to help everyone get themselves and their families out. For the most part, we succeeded.*

Some in our team refused to evacuate in the morning, and by the evening it was already too late. The territory was under artillery fire or was already under occupation. While most evacuated, some remained in occupied territory and had to stay there for a while, before they could move to safety. Some of them even tried to work from there and share some intelligence info with us, so we could pass it on to our Armed Forces. Was it perfect? Probably not. But we did our best to be there for the members of our team. The foundation was constant, honest, transparent, and caring communication. We responded to every request in our chat. Our HR called everyone who was in the territory close to the Russian Federation and asked what help was needed.

In a few days, when everything settled down and everyone who could - was evacuated, a new problem emerged: it was not easy to find housing for our employees and their families. Once this was resolved, a new problem appeared: the entire team was emotionally exhausted and could not work. This was especially true of sales and marketers, whose work is directly related to their mood and emotional state. We arranged for people to work part of their usual working week. We made clear that, whatever the result, they were safe for the next three months. We hired psychologists to help employees with their mental state. But the biggest and best result came from a daily online meeting where people could just chat and share their emotions. We called this "at the campfire". Everyone felt as if we just gathered peacefully around the campfire, in a friendly way, just to talk about the things that were on our minds. All this gave our team the much-needed feeling that they were taken care of: there was an island of stability in this crisis.

Alex and I tried to do something for team members that our parents did for us as children: We knew that if we needed it, we could go to our parents and they would solve any problem. That's what we tried to be for our employees - at any cost. After all, the team is the main value of any company, in Alex's and my opinion.

I won't lie - sometimes, the stress was unbearable. I wanted to cry and throw in the towel. But every time I felt like this, I kept to myself, so that no one would see it. I'm a human being - I had emotions that I needed to experience. But I only allowed myself to do this after the work was done and I had some time for myself. The rest of the time, you have to pack all your stress and emotions in a mental box to take care of later, at a more suitable time. To do that, I would remind myself of the responsibility I had for the people who were waiting for a solution from me. That was my main source of power. Then I managed to turn the sadness and anxiety into anger: a strong fury at the situation that allowed me to take action despite the difficulties. If you allow yourself to experience it, it gives you incredible strength.

Managing your mental state & leading your team

> *The most interesting thing was what happened to our sales. The first month, of course, there were almost none - everyone was focused on the invasion: evacuation, new housing, the hopeless mental state we were all in. But from the second month, sales began to recover at an incredible pace. In the third month, we were selling more than before the war. It was a payback we didn't expect. We explained to the team that the company critically needed to restore business operations and cash flow. We spent a lot of time communicating with the teams focused on marketing, development, sales, and support, and it paid off."*

Crises are never convenient. They are often messy and unpredictable and can make everybody stressed. In the most heated moments, feelings can take over. This can lead to personal conflicts and ineffective decisions. The role of a leader is to provide a safe environment for people, even in abnormal circumstances.

Recognize that everything is not within your control. Focus your energy on areas where you can make a difference and create change, allowing you to demonstrate positive development to the organization. In difficult times, even small positive changes will matter. Remind yourself of past challenges you've overcome or make positive affirmations (visualizations of a successful outcome) that reinforce your ability to handle the situation.

In the difficulty of the moment, you see opportunities. Among the mistakes, you've also noticed great achievements. Being hopeful means expressing confidence, optimism, and resilience in the face of crisis. You need to inspire others to do the same.

Dampen the emotional temperature: Rita McGrath[15]

In a podcast interview with Stoyan, Rita McGrath, Strategy Professor at Columbia Business School, referred to Thomas Kolditz and his book: "In Extremis Leadership"[16]. Kolditz was eager to study what he called "crisis professionals" - people who voluntarily put themselves in positions of greater danger. He explored what makes them succeed.

One of Kolditz's key conclusions was that in a crisis, it's the leader's job to dampen down the emotional temperature. A good leader doesn't act like the ones in the movies, who scream and slam phones down. According to McGrath, an effective leader assesses the situation and reflects on their options. They remain calm and let everyone take a breath, calm down, and take a step back. Rita calls it "absorbing uncertainty for people".

"So you don't have the answer right in the middle of a crisis. But what you can do is say, ok, here are the assumptions I'm making for now, here is what I expect you to behave like. And so you take the burden of uncertainty off your people so they can do whatever it is they need to do." As Kolditz says: *"We need to get people focused outside themselves."*

---

[15] Rita McGrath is a best-selling author, sought-after speaker, and longtime professor at Columbia Business School.

[16] "In Extremis Leadership" is a book written by retired army general officer and leadership coach Thomas A. Kolditz

> So, if they are in the middle of a dangerous situation and they are panicking you can say: *"Here is your job for the next two-and-a-half hours. Take that and move it from here to there. And if you do that, well, that will be a contribution to our success."* Get people focused outside themselves, on a meaningful task. Create clarity about the assumptions you are making and take away the burden of all that uncertainty.

Melissa Rosenthal, CMO of InsightTimer[17], a meditation and wellbeing mobile app with 27 million users, suggests a similar approach:

"Keep your team calm. Explain the challenge/the issue and focus on fixing it. There will be a retro in which you will be able to go back and discuss what went wrong, but at that moment, it's no politics, no blame: focus on fixing it.

Get everyone together who needs to be involved in the decision about how they are going to fix it and rally people together. That will not only create camaraderie, but people will be focused on the actual outcome, rather than screaming or throwing a fit, pointing out what's wrong.

Just focus on fixing it... And then you have a retro. You'll then understand: this is why that broke down. How do we prevent or fix it next time? What could we have done better? The retro is the time for that."

---

[17] *InsightTimer was founded in 2009 in Sydney, New South Wales. It solves everyday wellbeing needs for employees and teams. Advanced machine-learning models recommend relevant content and allow employees to track their mood and wellbeing, write a gratitude journal, sleep better and more.*

Protect your team. Have more frequent communications and check-ins. Make sure everyone is feeling well. You're likely to be under pressure and very busy, but you should still allocate time to be there for your people. Inspire honest conversations to understand what stresses everyone and what bothers them most. This also enables you to figure out what kind of support you can offer to take care of them and their mental well-being.

As we discussed in the previous chapter, a crisis might require downsizing. Even if you are able to keep your whole team, they might have to make an extra effort. It's easy to motivate your team to work hard and stay positive for a day or even a week. But what if you experience a "sustained crisis", it might take months of operating in "crisis mode". What if some of your best people leave? What if you have to delay salaries, but people still need to do their best and a little more?

Here comes another part of your job. Finding ways to remain positive and keep everyone motivated and engaged. Celebrate all the small wins and show gratitude to those who are with you on this journey. Gratitude alone won't be enough to keep your people motivated when their personal finances and lives have been impacted, but gratitude fuels the strength to let you and your team get through the crisis.

Staying positive and keeping your team engaged for a few months of crisis: QX[18]

Imagine that you've been building a product for over two years, and you and your team have survived two major crises (COVID-19 and a cash shortfall). Just as you are about to sign your first major client (a move that would solve all your current problems) your co-founder goes rogue. What would you do?

Zoran Nasteski, the co-founder and CEO of QX (formerly Qpick) lived through this and came out the other end as a survivor of a major startup crisis. QX is a Web3 Customer Experience and Loyalty platform that empowers retailers, brands, and shopping malls to transform digital impressions, footfall, and product boxes into digital assets and loyalty tokens, increasing engagement tenfold for clients. Zoran tells the story:

"For a very long time, I believed that my co-founder and I had a greater story than Steve Jobs and Wozniak, but I couldn't have been more wrong. We were a team that built a company from the ground up, but my technical co-founder considered the product to be his own and the sole foundation of our success.

His behavior and my naive ability to tolerate shady attitudes and red flags brought the company to collapse. It cost all of our employees their jobs. How did it come to this? We worked together for more than 4 years, even before starting Qpick. I noticed his attitude and behavior around our employees, and it scared me. However, I de-

---

[18] *QX is a technology company committed to transforming customer experiences and loyalty for brands, retailers, and shopping centers worldwide based in Wrocław, Poland in 2022.*

cided to not confront him, to avoid losing the key member in product development. This tolerance gave him more confidence. The toxic environment he created resulted in 99% of our team working closer to me, avoiding him. The company nevertheless progressed, attracting top talent, investors, media, and even potential customers, while the product turned into a maze that no other person could understand.

One day I challenged my co-founder and proposed a pivot: break down the product into a few parts. He just stood there silently. Then he went to our potential client, pitched the product and they decided to get on board. While I was in a meeting, my co-founder was pooling the data and bashing the product into a trash can. When I finally got the chance to talk to him, he said: 'This is my product and you will never succeed without it'.

Was this a crisis? Most definitely. Through my entrepreneurship journey, I developed a strong sense of accountability, but when things go downhill, you can feel hopeless. It took me over four months to get over it mentally, reorganize, and find people who were willing to work for free. We managed to save the company, the brand, and the designs, We also got rid of a pile of software nobody wanted to use. From this crisis I've managed to rebuild a strong company, keep my investors' trust, win back clients, and best of all, find the best co-founders ever.

When a crisis hits, we instantly focus on the problems, but most of the time things are in our heads. We should take care of ourselves first. Chill, get your mind straight, and then go back to work. Otherwise, depression will eat *your effectiveness. You will make poor decisions, leading to more failure.*

What I did to get things right and save the company:

- *I split tasks 50/50 between fixing internal problems and opportunity searching. This gave a perfect balance between re-organising and progressing*
- *I talked to ex-employees to get their perspective on the company, focusing on what they thought wasn't working, so I could make sure I was aware of our problems (and keep my ego in check)*
- *I talked to our employees twice a week on general subjects, to identify new leaders. This helped me find my next co-founding team*
- *I set up meetings with new candidates for product development every week, so we were ready in case we signed an opportunity*

How I kept myself sharp to combat stress and anxiety every day:

- *I woke up early, took a cold shower for two minutes, and went for a 30-40-minute walk in nature. I did intensive workouts and made sure I viewed morning sunlight for 5 minutes. Putting stress on my body kept my mind away from dark thoughts.*
- *My morning routine included audiobook listening or just listening to the sound of nature. This gave me a sense of deep connection to life and energy. It made it easier for me to see the business problems as something separate to my life.*
- *I talked to close friends more often to get their*

sympathy and guidance. This was really helpful in giving me motivation and courage.
- *I had long conversations with family members almost daily, on the phone or in person. This allowed me to complain and get sympathy which also brings support and motivation to continue (but if you do this: be aware of toxic family members)*

My main learnings from this crisis:
1. Never compromise your company culture and values. You can't tolerate negative behavior, even if someone has strong individual capabilities and skills.
2. Don't act emotionally in a crisis and always stay focused on the goal. This is the only way you will survive
3. Don't be afraid to start over again. This time, you're not starting from scratch, you're starting from experience.
4. Ask for help and you'll receive it."

Key Takeaways

• Effective leaders learn to remain calm and make rational decisions, even in the most stressful situations. Find your own reboot tools and take control of your emotions.

• To be well prepared to endure difficulties, focus on building the fundamentals. Take time daily to strengthen your body, your mind, and your support network. Lean on these in times of crisis.

• When a crisis hits, try your best to dampen the emotional temperature and absorb the uncertainty for your team. Be there for them and leave the "finger-pointing" aside. You will have time to review and reflect after the crisis is resolved.

• While going through a crisis, have frequent check-ins with your team. Make sure everyone is feeling heard and taken care of.

Opportunity Story

Have hope and keep goin: TALENTUNO / HROS[19]

Zsolt Kelliar is the co-founder and CEO of Talentuno, a crowdsourcing recruitment platform based in Hungary. Talentuno enables job seekers to connect with growing companies through personal networks.

In 2019, business was going strong. The company raised a €4 million Series A round and scaled the team to 80 employees. With 30-40% growth each quarter, the future seemed bright. Then, in March 2020, the COVID-19 pandemic hit. Suddenly 90% of the company's revenue was gone since uncertainty forces most companies to freeze or significantly cut hiring.

For several months, there was complete chaos for Zsolt and his team. Although they were working tirelessly, the situation didn't look hopeful.

They had to accept that they needed to lay people off to survive. After the layoffs, several further team members left. The company was down to 30-35 employees. The team focused on raising a Series B round to secure cash until the crisis is over. Despite many conversations with investors, funding stalled, too. Finally, they found a VC willing to back them. After 2-3 months of negotiations and term sheets signed, the VC backed off. It was a major setback, but

---

[19] *HROS is a company recruitment matchmaking platform, headquartered in Vienna, Austria.*

the team kept going.

Soon after, the situation almost repeated itself. A state-owned VC decided to invest. Negotiations went well. All paperwork was done, due diligence made and everything was ready. The board approved the transaction. At the very last minute, the VC pulled out.

Zsolt and the team couldn't believe it. The situation was really bad, with the company in debt to the tune of €700-800K. Without a miracle, it had 10 days left. The CFO, a former employee of Qualisoft, suggested setting up a meeting with his former employers. Having nothing to lose, Zsolt and his co-founder accepted. They presented their case, being fully transparent about the situation. Qualisoft liked what they saw and were interested in investing. But Talentuno needed the first €200 -300k within a few days to avoid bankruptcy. Qualisoft agreed to take the enormous risk to wire them the money, with one condition: The previous investors (State-owned VCs) who held around 40% of the company needed to come down to 5% and sell their shares for a pittance.

Zsolt immediately set up a meeting with them. He presented two options: see the company die in a few days or sell most of its shares, keeping just a fraction of its equity. They agreed to the latter. The miracle happened - they had enough funds to survive. The crisis created an opportunity for Talentuno to clear up its cap table.

A few months later, the situation looked much better. Clients came back. Cashflows became more consistent. In 2023 Talentuno merged with the Austrian company HROS. The two firms joined forces to transform the recruitment industry together. Despite all the setbacks, the founders never gave up. Eventually, they found a way out of a dire situation.

"If you believe in your vision, you shouldn't wrap up until it's over, " says Zsolt.

Final Remarks

Having to deal with a crisis is never a pleasant experience - but as a founder, you can be almost certain it will happen. Crises are messy, exhaustive, and likely to keep you up at night. Don't be discouraged.

Act fast. Minimize the damage. Mitigate the risk and ensure survival. Keep doing your best, and when feeling lost get back to your values and your purpose.

Even if it doesn't feel like it at the time, remember that a crisis will also yield many opportunities:
- Opportunities to grow your team
- Opportunities to develop as a leader
- Opportunities for new markets, product offerings, and business models

To finish up this book, we'd like to introduce you to a tool that can help you capture the opportunities:

Opportunity-Seizing Canvas: EXERCISE

To brainstorm ideas and opportunities you can use the following whiteboard exercise.

Bring your team together and follow these steps:

Step 1: Map
Internal resources:
- What skills & capabilities do we currently have in the team?
- What makes us unique / what are our superpowers?
- What tangible assets and resources can we use? (Technology, facilities, Intellectual property, pat-

ents)
- What intangible resources do we have? (Network of contacts, Reputation, Know-How, Background & experience, Passions)

Step 2: Identify
MARKET TRENDS & CHALLENGES:
- What market trends can we identify?
- Which industries/customer segments are struggling?
- What are the biggest pains/challenges our customers or potential customers have?

Step 3: Brainstorm
OPPORTUNITIES & SOLUTIONS
- What new opportunities can we identify to serve our customers?
- What new customer segments can we help?
- What solutions and products can we develop to get the most out of the situation?
- How can we innovate to better serve our customers' needs now, in terms of pricing/offering, customer experience or our overall approach?

Step 4: Curate
THE GOOD IDEAS
- Identify which ideas are worth taking forward
- Develop them further

"Never let a good crisis go to waste"
- *Winston Churchill*

Next steps

We hope to stay connected.

There are several ways to get in touch with the authors and their projects. First of all, connect with Stoyan and Cristobal on LinkedIn and share your thoughts about the book. And also feel free to check some of the links below.

The PERFORM movement
PerformNow.eu
Find free resources and additional materials.

Stoyan Yankov
www.stoyanyankov.com
Book Stoyan to speak at your next event, or lead a personalized workshop session for your team.

(Jose) Cristobal Alonso (Martin)
www.cristobalalonso.com
Keep track of Cristobal Alonso's publications - and why not check his cooking blog .-)

PERFORM in the Kitchen:
https://performinthekitchen.com/

Startup Wise Guys
www.startupwiseguys.com
Check out the programs of the leading B2B accelerator in Europe.

Productivity Mastery Podcast
https://stoyanyankov.com/podcast
Listen to inspiring podcast interviews with some of the world's most successful founders, business leaders, and bestselling authors.

The authors:

Stoyan's Linkedin

Stoyan Nikolaev Yankov

Stoyan Yankov is a former movie producer turned into a productivity & performance coach and professional speaker. He helped more than 550 companies across the globe to build strong, peak-performing teams through training, workshops, and coaching programs.

His clients include large international companies such as HP, Unicredit, Ramboll, DraftKings, and Centrica, high-growth scale-ups, and startup acceleration programs.

Stoyan is also the founder & host of the podcast Productivity Mastery, interviewing guests such as the

founder of Reebok. the founding president of Starbucks International, unicorn founders, and top-tier executives. During his career - Stoyan has interviewed over 250 of the most successful founders and business leaders on the planet, learning practical ideas and insights into what it takes to build a great team. As a speaker, Stoyan often gets invited to share knowledge and advice on the international stage at business and executive events. He has delivered keynotes in over 35 countries at major international conferences such as Web Summit, The Next Web, and TEDx. Stoyan is also an avid reader, podcast listener, and a very active LinkedIn user. (Make sure to add him as a contact and send a little note with your thoughts about the book). He holds an "MSc Finance" degree from Aarhus University - BSS.
https://stoyanyankov.com/

Cristobal's Linkedin

(Jose) Cristobal Alonso (Martin)

Cristobal Alonso is the definition of a global CEO. He is an experienced serial entrepreneur, a 3-time CEO,

a serial early-stage investor with more than 400 investments, and a global executive who has led teams and projects encompassing up to 500 people. He has lived and worked in 5 continents, 20+ countries, and 36 cities. Today he lives between Malaga and Copenhagen. Cristobal is CEO, "El Patron" and General Partner of Startup Wise Guys, the most active early-stage investor in Europe and Africa, investing in early-stage SaaS, Cyber Security & Defense, Sustainability, XR, Fintech, Proptech, and Web3 B2B startups. He is passionate about coaching startups on purpose & culture as well as funding and market engineering. Cristobal has extensive experience as the public face of media outreach campaigns and is a frequent keynote speaker at webinars, podcasts, and conferences around the world. He holds an MBA from INSEAD and has served as President of INSEAD's Global Entrepreneurship Club and the Spanish INSEAD Alumni Association. Cristobal is also a former professional basketball player, enjoys playing the piano, and shares his love for cooking and wine with as many guests as possible.
https://cristobalalonso.com/

Acknowledgments

Contributors:

To make this book practical and relevant, we included examples, quotes, and recommendations from a large number of successful founders and business leaders. Many of them we interviewed individually to find the untold learnings and stories. Others, we were inspired by and quoted in the book. Nevertheless, we are grateful for everyone who contributed to making this book happen.

In alphabetical order:

Alexandru Stan 🇷🇴
Founder & CEO of Tekpon 🇷🇴
https://tekpon.com/

Albert Camus 🇫🇷
French philosopher and author

Anders Thomsen 🇩🇰
Co-founder & CEO of SlideHub 🇩🇰
https://slidehub.io/

Andrew Tarvin 🇺🇸
Author of "Humor that Works" 🇺🇸
https://drewtarvin.com/

Ben Horowitz 🇺🇸
Investor & Author of "The Hard Thing About Hard Things"

Boris Krastev 🇧🇬
CEO and co-founder of RemoteMore 🇺🇸
https://remotemore.com/

Braveen Kumar 🇮🇳
Author
https://www.braveenkumar.com/

Brené Brown 🇺🇸
Professor at University of Houston 🇺🇸
https://brenebrown.com/

Brian Chesky 🇺🇸
Co-founder and CEO of Airbnb 🇺🇸
https://www.airbnb.com/

Christo Popov 🇧🇬
Founder and CEO of FastTrack 🇧🇬
https://fasttrack-growth.com/

George Stalk Jr. 🇺🇸
Author, Vice-president, and Director of The Boston Consulting Group 🇺🇸

Georgi Malchev 🇧🇬
founder of XploraBG 🇧🇬
https://xplora.bg/

German Coppola 🇪🇸
CEO of YUMIWI 🇪🇸
https://yumiwi.com/

Heini Zachariassen 🇫🇴
CEO of Vivino 🇩🇰
https://www.vivino.com/

202

Hiten Shah 🇺🇸
Co-founder & CEO at Nira 🇺🇸
https://nira.com/

Howard Behar 🇺🇸
Former president of Starbucks International 🇺🇸
https://www.starbucks.com/

Howard Schulz 🇺🇸
Former CEO of Starbucks 🇺🇸
https://www.starbucks.com/

Ilma Tiki 🇱🇹
Co-founder of Mailer Lite 🇱🇹
https://www.mailerlite.com/

Ivan Kaunov 🇺🇦
Co-founder of Finmap 🇺🇦
https://www.finmap.online/

Jevgenij Polonis 🇱🇹
CEO and co-founder of GoRamp 🇱🇹
https://www.goramp.com/

Joe Foster 🇬🇧
Founder of Reebok 🇬🇧
https://www.reebok.com/

Jon Gordon 🇺🇸
Leadership author, consultant, and speaker
https://jongordon.com/

Jose Leopoldo Alonso 🇪🇸
Cristobal's father

Kai Schukowski 🇩🇪
General Manager at Kempinski Hotels 🇱🇹
https://www.kempinski.com/

Kate Williams 🇺🇸
CEO at 1% for the Planet 🇺🇸
https://www.onepercentfortheplanet.org/

Liudas Kanapienis 🇱🇹
CEO and co-founder, ONDATO
https://ondato.com/

Lubomila Jordanova 🇧🇬
CEO and co-founder of PlanA 🇩🇪
https://plana.earth/

Malcolm Gladwell 🇬🇧
Journalist, author, and public speaker
https://www.gladwellbooks.com/

Marian Temelkov 🇧🇬
CEO of Dynamis Group 🇬🇧
https://dynamisgroup.com/

Maris Dagis 🇦🇹
CEO of Sellfy 🇦🇹
https://sellfy.com/

Marilyn Zakhour 🇱🇧
Founder and CEO of Cosmic Centaurs 🇦🇪
https://www.cosmiccentaurs.com/

Merilin Hehir 🇪🇪
People and operations expert at Single Earth 🇪🇪
https://www.single.earth/

Martin Vares 🇪🇪
CEO of Fractory 🇪🇪
https://fractory.com/

Melissa Rosenthal 🇺🇸
Former CCO of ClickUp 🇺🇸
https://clickup.com/

Michelle Gielan 🇺🇸
Broadcaster and psychology researcher
https://michellegielan.com/

Momchil Kyukurchiev 🇧🇬
Co-founder of Leanplum 🇺🇸
https://www.leanplum.com/

Nazar Hembara 🇺🇦
CEO and founder of BotsCrew 🇺🇦
https://botscrew.com/

Oksana Gorbunova 🇺🇦
CEO and co-founder of BazaIT 🇺🇦
https://bazait.com/

Patrick Bet David 🇺🇸
Author of "Choose your Enemies Wisely"
https://www.patrickbetdavid.com/

Patrick Collins 🇱🇹
Sales coach and CEO of Prospect Labs 🇱🇹
https://www.theprospectlabs.com/

Patrick Lencioni 🇺🇸
Author of "The Five Dysfunctions of a Team"
www.tablegroup.com

Peter Drucker 🇺🇸
Management guru

Rita McGrath 🇺🇸
Strategy Professor at Columbia Business School 🇺🇸
https://www.ritamcgrath.com/

Robert Mckee 🇺🇸
Author & Screenwriter
https://mckeestory.com/

Sergiu Negut 🇷🇴
Co-founder & CSO at FintechOS 🇷🇴
https://fintechos.com/

Shane Hurlbut 🇺🇸
Hollywood Cinematographer
https://www.filmmakersacademy.com/

Shawn Achor 🇺🇸
Author and speaker
https://www.shawnachor.com/

Steli Efti 🇺🇸
Founder at Close.com 🇺🇸
https://www.close.com/

Stephen Covey 🇺🇸
Management consultant and author of "The Seven Habits of Highly Effective People"

Steve Cadigan 🇺🇸
Linkedin's First CHRO 🇺🇸
https://stevecadigan.com/

Toms Niparts 🇱🇻
Co-founder and CEO of JeffApp 🇪🇸
https://www.jeff-app.com/

Tracy Brower 🇺🇸
Journalist
https://tracybrower.com/

Victor Folmann 🇩🇰
COO at Metafy 🇺🇸
https://metafy.gg/

Victor Sanchez 🇨🇱
Co-founder & CTO of SkillMapper 🇫🇷
https://skillmapper.com/

Viktoria Nalyvaiko 🇺🇦
CEO and co-founder of BazaIT 🇺🇦
https://bazait.com/

Viktoriya Vasilenko 🇺🇸/🇺🇦
CEO of Knowledge Gate Group 🇩🇰
https://www.knowledgegategroup.com/

Zane Bojare 🇱🇻
Communications Consultant

Zoran Nasteski 🇲🇰
Co-founder and CEO of QX 🇲🇰
https://qx.ventures/

Zsolt Kelliar 🇭🇺
Co-founder and COO of HROS 🇭🇺
https://hros.io/

Special Thanks

We would like to thank everyone who helped us to make this book come to life.

Thank you to our editor Jessica Sandin for the incredible commitment to lifting our standards up, providing us with the necessary "tough love" within a few rounds of feedback, and for improving the language. Thank you to Billy Lyell, for keeping up with us and jumping to support any possible tasks that were needed to keep the book on track. Thank you to our designer Simona Veselinova for creating the visual style, all the graphics, and the layout of the book. To Anna Nikolova for your mentoring, and for helping us bring the visual style to the next level. Thank you Yoana Zoteva for your enormous effort in pushing us to make the book better, for all the proofreading, sourcing, and constructive feedback.

Thank you also to everyone else who contributed to the book in one way or another by providing feedback, sharing advice, helping us to set up interviews with the founders, and last but not least supporting us to keep going and making a better book: Nicoleta Pirvu, Razvan Suta, Austin Nicholas, Boris Borisov, Eleonora Petrova, Gergana Todorova, Veselin Tonov, Bozdhidar Bogdanov, Patrick Mork, Auste Silkaityte.

And if for some reason we forgot to mention you, make sure to let us know so we can include you in the next edition.

Did you enjoy the book?

Get a copy of our first book and learn how to apply the PERFORM methodology to build a strong team with a productive culture.

Scan here

to get your copy

Drop us a line and let us know how you liked it.

Printed in Poland
by Amazon Fulfillment
Poland Sp. z o.o., Wrocław

36821592R10121